Mal Paharia Culture at the Crossroad

Mal Paharia Culture at the Crossroad

Amitabha Sarkar
Samira Dasgupta

AGAM

AGAM KALA PRAKASHAN
NEW DELHI

First Published 2011

ISBN : 978-81-7320-105-9

Published by
Dr. Agam Prasad, M.A., Ph.D., Diploma in Museology
For **Agam Kala Prakashan**
34, Central Market, Ashok Vihar,
Delhi-110 052.
Ph. : 011-27212195, 65688806-7
Fax : 011-27212195
E-mail : agambooks@gmail.com, info@agamkala.com
Website : www.agamkala.com

Composed by
Elegant Printographics
319, IIIrd Floor, R. G. Complex,
Sector-14, Rohini, Delhi-110085

Printed by
Chawla Offset
Delhi-110052.

Printed in India

Foreword

Anthropological and more specifically, ethnographic research has been important in illuminating specific communities closeted in their natural setting to come to terms with rapid changes that have taken place in their land and that have assumed a global character. There is probably an element o predictability in this type of research in that it tries to stress upon the persistence of the local in the face of the "global". From anbother perspective, the very discourse of local vs. global is more unpredictable than one could possibly think it to be. This particularly applies to the local knowledge, which is never homogenised to produce a "monoculture" representing a universal form pursuing the local way of managing the material environment and has a positive value because it highlights the need to preserve such a knowledge system, from which the Western intellectual tradition can learn for its own benefit. For a long time, the West-based tradition preferred to ignore the utility of such a system. Even in our own knowledge system there was hardly any place for conservation or sustainable development programmes by making profitable use of the local experience. Only recently, we have come to realise that successul and sustainable conservation of natural resources can be achieved by the induction of local knowledge and practices o nature ingrained in culture. This calls for adoption of an approach that would allow the local people with a long tradition o living with nature to cultivate their own knowledge system for the conservation of material environment. Of late, the indigenous people themselves have become aware of the fact that they have inalienable rights over the natural environment they are in close association with. Their culture which provides the basis for the localised form of resistance against developers who are out to encroach upon their rights. The predicaments of such a group of people are not all their own creation. The economic burdens they are to carry today are rather thrust upon them by the developers. The whole question of development now assumes a political ecological dimension focussing on the interrelations among culture, environment, development and socio-political movements initiated by specific communities. The dominating trend is, however, to manage the differential modes of access to resources on a global scale and here the forlorn voices of small indigenous groups are rarely heard.

Even in the case of a primitive tribal group (PTG) like the Mal Paharia a process of internal differentiation has started working in their system which may be attributed to the indirect effect of globalisation, obviously, it has weakened the compact cohesive structure of the tribe, which goes to the advantage of globalists. In a situation when the state-centrists are at loggerheads with the globalists, the ultimate sufferer is the community. When a primitive tribal group like the Mal Paharia are involved in such a tangle, their sustaining power has been put to severe test.

Amitabh Sarkar and Samira Das Gupta have made a sincere attempt to catch the traditional spirit defining the hard points of Mal Paharia culture and at the same time identify the areas of change and adaptation. What transpires is that globalisation has spread none, not even the Mal Paharia. From an altogether different perspective, the Mal Paharia represent a classic example of change and continuity. They have still been using symbols to reproduce their culture, but can do nothing more than looking on helplessly the way their cultural experience has been marginalised with the passage of time. The traditional bent of mind with which they so grudgingly guard their culture has started giving way to the onslaught of rapidly expanding global power.

Rajat Kanti Das

Rajat Kanti Das
U.G.C. Emiritus Fellow
in Anthropology,
Dept. of Anthropology,
Vidyasagar University,
Midnapore, West Bengal

Preface

The anthropologists now-a-days in our country are becoming arm chair anthropologist and not interested in prolong field investigation while, they mainly depend on secondary sources and net surfing, while the wide horizon of anthropology has a vast scope in understanding society, culture, people, and their problems through in-depth study by prolong field work with the help of tools and techniques in anthropology and it has achieved a special status in the field of anthropology and other allied disciplines of social science.

With the advancement of technology and flow of money the inter-personal relationship of society is being changed; the marginalized and grass-root level people are not beyond such wave. Through the tenets of globalization, primarily which means, connectivity and rising interdependence of world society into a single whole, under this context how the Mal Paharia –a Primitive Tribal Group of Damin-i-Koh area of Jharkhand are becoming empowered and increasing cultural interaction with the outsiders, although they are maintaining their age-old belief system at their forest habitat where their life and culture is cherished. Further, in spite of various waves of globalization they still have full faith on traditional medicinal plants of their vicinity during ailment. But this knowledge bank is eroding fast and most of those had already been lost due to wave of modernization and globalization as well as the rapid spread of foreign technology and money introduced or imported from outside. The new means of communication at their area also empowers Mal Paharia for enhancing cultural interaction with the outsiders. But it does not imply the total change of traditional system by a new one.

The interest of this sort of empirical study among the Mal Paharia was developed during field work from December,2006 to January,2007 by the Anthropological Survey of India, Kolkata in connection with the project "Syncretism in India". During the period of intensive fieldwork we had ample opportunity to have a close observation on the life and culture of the Mal Paharia tribe and their neighbouring- Santal. The present treatise is based on direct involvement of field investigation. Door to door household survey was made and also witnessed good number of their ritual activities, punishment and *jat-bhitar* ritual in connection with violation of customary law, also observed the use of herbal medicines etc. Moreover, collection of empirical data in various locales also suggests for variation and cross-cultural interaction as well as validation of collected data.

At the very outset, we owe a deep sense of gratitude to all the informants of the studied villages, Dumka District Administration especially, Deputy Commissioner, Deputy Development Commissioner and District Welfare Officer—Mr. Dasharath Raut for their full fledged co-operation in collecting data as well as to accord permission to visit various Mal Paharia villages in remote corner. We consider it as our sacred duty to convey our sincere regards to all of them.

We also express our thanks to Dr. Satyendra Singh, Director, Agrarian Assistance Association (AAA), Mr. Tarakeshwar Singh of AAA, Kalicharan Deheri, Mal Paharia (Retd. Under Secretary, Legislative Assembly of

Bihar, Patna,), Rajendra Deheri and Kapil Deheri of Madhuvan village, Baburji Hembram(Santal) , Madhuvan village Pradhan and Neplal Singh of Upar Murgathali village for their active support in collection of data. We also extend our heartfelt thanks to Shri, Asok Mukhopadhyay who also accompanied during our empirical study but with a different research assignment among the Mal Paharia. We are grateful to Sri, Santosh Pathak and Debashis Biswas of the Anthropological Survey of India, Kolkata for their sincere effort in typing the manuscript in the computer as well as digital conversion of our coloured photographs.

We are also grateful to the Director, Anthropological Survey of India for his encouragement in publishing fundamental empirical research work. Further, it would be unethical if we do not acknowledge Dr. Biman K Dasgupta, ex. Deputy Director of the Anthropological Survey of India with due respect, under whose guidance the present volume is prepared.

Further, special thanks are due to Dr. Agam Prasad of Agam Kala Prakashan- an esteemed publication house of Delhi, for the specific care and attention given by him to bring out the volume in such a short time. Lastly, we think our effort would meet a sensational success if requisite attention is coined from the planners of the country as well as researchers and NGOs in this field to understand the situation for sustainable development.

List of Plates

Contents

1

Introduction

With the advancement of technology and consequent flow of money the society is being changed and as a result, even in the grass root level, that is village level, the traditional inter personal relation is also affected. A vast section of Indian tribal people, mostly marginalized due to their forest background have three broad aspects of their expression of culture (Vidyarthi, 1963) namely, **Nature**, stands for geographical environment, while **Man** represents the society and the **Spirit** signifies the supernatural world, are not the exception. With the progress of time, various agents of culture are borrowed from neighbouring cultures that make a traditional marginalized group to adapt the new situation and as a result culture change occurs among the group. Changes are found in their material, social and religious life as well as ideational aspects of culture like, ethos, value system, world-view, ideals, belief system and the like.

The fundamental base of social-culture behaviour lies in man-to-man interaction; the material culture on the other hand, is essentially an outcome of man's interaction with environment. Man's capacity and equipment to exploit the environment determine the level of technology – a major ingredient of material culture. The nature of material objects and material way of living, possessed by a group of people are also, many times, considerably directed by the environments around.

The impact of Hindus on the tribals has been a long drawn process and it has attracted the attention of a quite a good number of anthropologists (Sahay, 1967), Risley (1891) is of the opinion that most of the lower castes of today have a tribal origin and he describes four processes by which transformation of a tribe into caste is effected. Elwin (1941) on the basis of his study among the tribes of Madhya Pradesh classified them into three types in terms of their acculturation.

Griffiths (1946) while talking about the process of Hinduization in 'Kol' tribe expressed that they are apparently forming a miniature caste system within the tribe somewhat modeled after Hindu castes.

Srinivas (1952) acclaimed the concept of 'Sanskritisation' implies that the rites and beliefs of castes occupying the lower rungs of the caste ladder as well as the rites and beliefs of outlying communities hidden away in the forest clothed mountains of India have been subjected to Sanskritisation.

Bailey (1960) while distinguishing a tribe from caste in his study of highland Orissa mainly taken political and economic criteria into consideration and feels the need of postulating a continuum at two ends of which stands a tribe and a caste.

Bose (1961) taking the case of Juangs of Central Orissa, who were once hunter-gatherers, says that they have slowly submitted to their Hindu neighbours and sought new occupations. Sinha (1962) on the basis of historical and ethnographic studies of the Bhumij puts forward the concept of 'tribal-Rajput continuum'. With a number of examples he has discussed as to how the various tribal groups of Central India like Bhumij, Gond, Munda have been influenced by the formation of state in their respective territory, which appears to have emerged mainly through internal development of a tribal base.

Vidyarthi (1968) analysing the processes and pattern of transformation taking place in tribal India, in general and points out two sets of processes: -

(i) Traditional and
(ii) Modern

The traditional process is characterized by the impact of certain traditions of the dominant regional society on the tribal group and has long been in operation and led to the resultant concepts like Hinduization, Sanskritization, Tribe caste Continuum, Tribal – Rajput Continuum, Revitalisation, etc., while on the other hand, the modern process includes such factors like Christianity, Industrialization, Urbanization, Developmental Schemes, Modernization, Advancement of education, Penetration of communication and local administration (like three tier panchayat system) etc. Thus modern processes are fast, induced planned and sponsored and in many way characterized by 'imposition' and not 'selection' while the traditional processes stands just in contrast to it.

Christianity is another important factor of culture change in tribal India in general and the tribal Jharkhand in particular. Sahay's (1976) work on impact of Christianity among the Oraon clearly reflects that transformation taken place in the life and culture of the Oraon and also puts forth five cultural processes through which transformations taking place in the life of the tribal converts and can be understood and these processes are – Oscillation, Scrutinization, Combination, Indigenisation, and Retro version.

There are many apprehensions about globalisation. It is not a recent phenomenon but certainly it has some kind of specific role in the present day. To our mind globalisation means primarily- **connectivity and increasing interdependence of world societies into a single whole**. Thus, in view of penetration of this force that involves free flow of trade, capital, and information which led growth and welfare of society in wider way and ultimately affected the worldwide living pattern.

Ralph Linton (1936) told that, primordial human societies are governed by principles wherein every member shares everything thus the degree of sharing is in totality. Then through the process of internal differentiation the specialisation arises, when such differentiated society comes in contact with extraneous sources for exchange of information and incentive, the degree of differentiation multiplies. Leaving to a high degree what Linton calls '**areas of alternatives or multiplicity of option**'. Globalisation is a contemporary concept. It is nothing but magnification of the process-identified as expression of globalisation.

In the present day context globalisation refers to increasing interdependence in between world societies in various worldwide issues, namely, trade, finance, communication, travel, culture, ideas, disaster management as well as to control and eradicate the violence and insurgency. Among these, the most important dimension of globalisation are-economic globalisation, cultural globalisation and political globalisation. Appadurai (2000) has shown this connectivity as world of flows – (i) ethnoscapes, (ii) mediascapes, (iii) technoscapes, (iv) financescapes and (v) ideoscapes

It is true that revolutionary changes in technology, transport, and communication have altogether altered the economy, ways of life of the people at all corners of this planet and converted the world into a 'global village'. The global culture is not just a higher version of local cultures rather it is the cultural interaction in the global and local level (Mondal, 2006).

In the era of cultural globalisation the basic concept of culture as "shared patterns of learned belief and behaviour constituting the total life ways of a group of people; the totality of tools, acts, thoughts and institutions of any given human population" has also been changing. Culture as a particularistic and localized phenomenon is fast becoming out-dated with the increasing penetration of external elements of non-integrated traits accumulated through the process of globalisation. The boundaries of culture proved to be quite flexible. With the increasing process of globalisation, the concept of culture no longer remains the same as before (Mondal, 2006). Globalisation also applauds for cultural and social ethnic identities of the local people. With **the tenets of globalisation the local people are becoming empowered and increasing cultural interaction with the outsiders**. Thus in this era of cultural globalisation the issue of cultural imperialism cannot be ignored and in this context media and communication are playing the key role.

Under this backdrop the present investigation is carried out among the Mal Paharia- a Primitive Tribal Group of Jharkhand, India who are nourished in the afforested hilly terrain of Rajmahal hills in Dumka district of Jharkhand. The term 'primitive' in the present days has been subjected to invite criticism from a number of scholars especially from anthropologists because many communities are labelled as primitive irrespective of diverse varieties in socio-cultural life. There are altogether 75 PTGs (Primitive Tribal Group) as per as Government of India notification dated 27th April 1980. The denotative marker for identifying, a tribal group as PTG are- communication, economy, population size, social life as well as personality , level of education and use of technology on which their subsistence activities are conditioned. Under this backdrop the present authors feel to substitute the term as **Virgin or Vulnerable Tribal groups for PTG.**

The present empirical study is carried out among the Mal Paharia under the broad umbrella of "Syncretism in India" project. Syncretism refers blending of cultural traits, religious belief system and also facilitates the co-existence of various cultural elements into an ongoing historical process (Das, 2007) and to achieve such process one has to pass through various phases. As a result community has to face an environment of changing perspective. Globalisation has become a recent phenomenon, which has varied dimensions mentioned earlier. This may be comparable with Vidyarthi's (1968) idea of modern processes of change. In fact, all the tenets of globalisation are agents for culture change and this may also be comparable with Vidyarthi's model (1968) of culture change.

Considering the dynamics of culture change the Mal Paharia tribe of Dumka, Jharkhand are studied who not only lead life of their own tradition in traditional abode of hilly- forest terrain of Rajmahal hills, also known as *Damin-i- koh*, where spiritual world is the root of their belief system, but also adapted modern technology for their livelihood. The present treatise contains an attempt to examine the nature of culture change in 21st century especially on religious belief systems, rituals as well as adaptation of new technology for survival and sustainable living among the Mal Paharia tribe of Rajmahal hills, Dumka district of Jharkhand state.

Mal Paharia is one of the tribes who live in a geographically difficult area where they always have a feeling of insecurity and uncertainty or less predictability. In fact Mal Paharia is a separate group of the tribe Paharia. Paharia is a blanket term for three separate tribes namely, Sauria Paharia, Kumbharbhag Paharia and Mal Paharia.All of the three are endogamous groups and confined to their habitat in *Damin–i–koh* (a Persian word means skirt of the hills) area of erstwhile Santhal Pargana district, which is now divided into Dumka, Pakur, Deoghar, Sahebgunj, Godda, and Jamtara districts.

Methodology

Standard anthropological tools and techniques such as, household census survey, genealogies to understand their change of occupation, reasons of death, rate of literacy, inter village linkages, ownership pattern of land, type of land owned and its tenure pattern, cereal produced, emic view of classification of land and accordingly its use, traditional wisdom in view of their agricultural practices, Brahmanical impact on marriage as well as induction of modern medical facility since their birth, case histories as well as focussed interview etc. are applied in data collection.

Selection of the Universe

The present study is carried out among Mal Paharia of Madhuvan village of Dumka district of Jharkhand. The intensive empirical data are collected from this village while to substantiate our base line data and for the sake of controlled comparison we have selected Gando village (erstwhile Gando estate of MalPaharia), Upar Murgathali village, close to Dumka block head quarter and Asansol village – very close to Dumka town and airstrip of the district. With the help of empirical observations especially qualitative data and controlled comparison of the studied village a changing perspective of Mal Paharia is being presented.

2

Ethno – Historical Background

The Paharia, both Mal Paharia and Sauria Paharia and Kumbharbhag Paharia are usually confined their habitat in Damin-i-koh area of erstwhile Santal Pargana district, which is now divided into Dumka, Pakur, Sahebgunj, Godda, Deoghar, and Jamatara districts. For presenting an account of ethno-historical background the researchers intend to initiate their discussion from **undivided** Santal Pargana district.

The district may be divided into three natural divisions. One is the hilly portion stretching from the bank of the Ganges in the north to the border of West Bengal in the south. It contains the Rajmahal hills and other hilly ranges and covers the entire *Damin* area. The hills and slopes are covered with forests – once dense but scanty now. The valleys have cultivable land, yielding mostly paddy. The second portion consists of the uplands, undulations, long ridges and depressions. It covers almost half of the district. Deoghar, Jamtara and parts of Godda, Dumka and Pakur subdivision fall within this region. This area has plenty of fertile lands and is intensively cultivated. There are high hills with lofty peaks viz. Tieur (2505 ft) and Phuljore

(2311 ft) in Deoghar subdivision and Masanjore in Dumka subdivision. The third region is a narrow strip of low fertile, alluvial plain lying between the Ganges and the hills running along loop railway line of the Eastern Railway.

The principal range in the district is Rajmahal Hills, which rise abruptly to some 1000-2000 ft. on the southern bank of the river Ganga. These hill stretch southward almost upto the Bengal border and form the backbone of the district – Santal Pargana. These hill ranges enclose between them about 5120 sq.km. of hilly tract, 3471 sq.km. of which is known as *Damin-i-koh.*

Damin-i-koh (a Persian word) means 'skirts of the hills'. It covers the area of Rajmahal, Pakur, Godda and Dumka sub-divisions. This land has been regarded by the

British Government as a reserve for the aboriginal races of the district and the intrusion of non-aboriginal called *dikku* has always been kept within the narrowest limit. The tract it covers consists of hills surrounded by flat country with fertile valleys lying, in some instance between parallel ranges. The valleys lying at the foot of the hills are well – watered by streams, cultivated and inhabited mostly by the Santal.

The record reveals that the earliest inhabitants are Maler (Sauria Paharia) who are found in the north of Rajmahal Hills; While Mal Paharia in the south and west of the Rajmahal hills engaged themselves as robbers and cattle lifters (Prasad and Singh, 1989). It is also reported that the authentic history of the Santal Parganas is said to begin with the rule of the Muslim when their troops marched to and from Bengal through the *Teliagarhi pass*. This pass, which was called the 'key of Bengal' due to strategic location of numerous hills. The region gained importance with establishment of Rajmahal as the capital of Bengal in 1592. After 1660 the capital was shifted to Dacca and the importance of Rajmahal dwindled. In the famine of 1770, the Paharias drove away the Ghatwals and the entire plains at the foot of hills laid at their mercy. Even the government mail runners, who in those days passed along the skirts of hills, by way of Rajmahal and *Teliagarhi pass*, were frequently robbed and murdered at the foot of the hills. Plunder, no doubt was the main object, but good number of their inroads were in the first instance instigated by the landholders, who were in the habit of offering the Paharias as free passage through their own lands, on condition that they ravaged those of the neighbouring Zamindars (Prasad and Singh, 1989).

During the tenure as collector of Bhagalpur in 1776 Augustus Cleveland informed 'the hills people are generally employed for plundering by the Ghatwals and Zamindari officers'. It has been almost a general custom with the low country inhabitants of Sultanabad, Rajshahi (now in Bangladesh) and Birbhum to employ the hill people in plundering each other's village. On the attention of Warren Hastings who rose a special corps under Captain Brooke sometimes during 1772-75. The disturbed tract i.e. the north of Santal pargana and south of Munger and Bhagalpur – the *Jungle Tarai,* was placed under captain Brooke as its Military Governor and with a number of successful expeditions in different parts of the hills succeeded and won the confidence of the Paharias and induce them to come down and settle in the cultivable lands below the hills. Since then the light of civilization in the Rajmahal hills are enlightened gradually.

In 1774 Captain Browne took charge of the *Jungle Tarai*. He introduced a scheme, known as the Hill system under which the hills were divided into different divisions called *parganas* or *tappas* each under a chief called Sardar. The people themselves were settled in village, each of which claimed a separate hill or range of hills and was presided over by a village chief or headman called *manjhi*. Browne proposed that this system of chiefs should be recognized and their services should be enlisted for the preservation of peace and order. All transactions with the hills people were to be carried on through *sardars* and *manjhis*. He firmly believed that the circulation of money in the hills was the most likely bait to ensure the attachment of the chiefs and at the same time nothing was more conducive to the civilization of the inhabitants as to employ a number of them in the services of the government. In 1782 the Paharias were enrolled in the corps of Archers or Hills Corps, later known as the Bhagalpur Hill Ranges, whom Cleveland used in pacifying their brethren.

With the Paharias cool down and retired to the hills there started Santal immigration in large number during last quarter of 18th century from Manbhum, Barahabhum, Chotanagpur, Hazaribagh, Midnapur, Dalbhum, Bankura, Birbhum etc. and settled out of clearing forest the low fertile land, which was once the dwelling place of these Paharia. The history of the Damin-i-koh is linked up with the struggle of the Paharias for freedom in the early days of British period. Being the stronghold of the Santals the Damin area had become the nerve center of the Santal resurrection in 1855.

According to Census of 1901 the population of the Damin-i-koh was 358,294, of whom no less than 226,540 were Santals and according to the 1931 census, the total population of Damin-i-koh is 411,677 of whom 242,647 are Santals who chiefly occupy the valleys and plain area portion of the estate. The next most numerous communities consist of the Paharias, of whom there are two branches – the Maler and the Mal Paharias. The former are found in the northern half of the estate in Rajmahal, the northern hills of Pakur and in Godda north of Borkabandh Bunglow. The latter occupy the Dumka portion of the Damin-i-koh, the Borokabandh Bunglow of Godda and south of Pakur. The Paharia villages are usually situated on the tops of the ridges and around the homesteads are the village *bari* lands extending to the brow of the hills. This area of homestead and cultivation is cut off from the lands, which the Santals occupy, by steep declivities, on portions of which the Paharias usually practise *kurao* cultivation (O'Malley, 1938 p.37)

Government has always regarded the Damin-i-koh as a reserved area for the aboriginal races of the district and intrusion of non-aborigines or foreigners, called *dikkus*, has always been restricted within the narrowest limits. It is, therefore, laid down that foreigners must not ordinarily be permitted to hold land within the boundaries of the Damin, and any one who happens to be improperly admitted is liable to be evicted, unless there is good cause to the contrary. In the course of Mr. Mc Pherson's settlement it was found that the average *dikku* holding was 4.47 acres while the average non-*dikku* holding was 6.89 acres (O' Maller, 1910, p.371).

It is also reported that Sankara – an estate in the Dumka sub-division extending over 80 sq.miles and comprising 109 villages. The estate appears to have been granted as a *lakhiraj* property to one Joy Singh by Asadulla Jaman Khan, who was Raja of Nagar in Birbhum in 18th century.

In 1840 it was resumed by the government and temporarily settled with the heirs of Joy Singh. In 1845 it was settled with Digbijay Singh, grandson of Sumar Singh who was grandson of Jay Singh too. Digbijay Singh was killed during the Santal insurrection of 1855 on the eastern embankment of a tank close to his house at Gando; the estate was then taken under the management of 'Court of Wards', which management still continues and was farmed out to Mr. G.H. Grant of Bhagalpur for a period of ten years from May 1856 to April, 1866; on the expiry of which the lease was renewed for another five years. Later Siva Sundari, the daughter of Digbijay Singh up till the date of her death at her family residence at Gando in year 1928, held the estate. After her death, her sons – Babu Hari Narain Singh and Babu Bholanath Singh became joint proprietors of the Estate. The former was adjudged a lunatic by the District court and the latter was realized that he would not be able to manage the property if left to him, applied and was declared to be disqualified proprietor and the court of wards retained charge of the whole estate. During 1933 Babu Bholanath Singh died and a dispute as to succession to the Estate is pending decision before the court. The members of the family call themselves Kumbharbhag Paharias and are believed to be of the same stalk as the Mal Paharias in the Dumka sub-division, amongst whom they have a considerable number of relatives. The estate derives its name from the village of Sankara, once the family residence, which lies in the Damin-i-koh, on the northern side of the river Brahmani, which separates the two estates. It is said that before the family settled at Gando they used to live at Pathaithan, where they migrated from Brindabon. The family also appears to have lived for a time at Murgathali on the Punasi Hills and before that at Dighi near the Singhin Hills. The later hills are closely connected with the tradition of the family and the family diety *Singh bahini* (rider of the lion), one of the names of the ten-armed Durga, is supposed to reside in a cave of them. Human sacrifices used to be offered to her, the last rite of this nature being performed under the orders of Prithi Singh, an uncle of Digbijay Singh (O'Malley, 1910, p.406).

Record also reveals that Paharias settled under a chief called Chand Sardar of Sultanbad pargana of the then Pakur sub-division within the jurisdiction of Maheshpur and Pakuria Police station. Chand Sardar used to live at a place about 6 miles away to the north of Maheshpur, which was known as Chandpur and still witnessed with old records and maps, but the present name of the village is Amlagachi. It is also reported that Maheshpur family of Sultanabad was conquered by two brothers – Abu Singh and Baku Singh and in alliance with Raja of Kharagpur defeated all the zamindars of the country. The elder brother – Baku Singh became ruler of the greater part of the tract, thus conquered and established his capital at Maheshpur. He was the founder of the Maheshpur Raj family, which is still in possession of Sultanabad. The younger brother Abu Singh took what was left and reclaimed a large area of hill and jungle. The two brothers, having secured themselves in possession, obtained recognition from the Nawab of Bengal, to whom Baku Singh sent every year some forest produce as tribute. While Abu Singh settled among the Paharias and is said to have married a Paharia woman (O'Malley, 1938, p.408). Since then Paharia especially Mal Paharia claim their ancestry from warrior or Rajput Gharana.

From the above discussion on their heritage it can be revealed that Mal Paharia may be a section of down trodden strata of the then Hindu fold having landed property but due to passage of time now they are classified as Scheduled Tribe especially PTG which is purely a political connotation.

3

Mal Paharia At Home: Villages under Study

Settlement Area

The Mal Paharia are mainly concentrated in Dumka district and local administrators identify them as Paharia who are one of the Primitive Tribal Group of Jharkhand. According to Risley (1981 reprinted), the Mal Paharias are a Dravidian tribe inhabiting the Ramgarh Hills of the erstwhile Santal Parganas. Until recently they live by hunting, gathering and *Kurao* (shifting hills cultivation). Dalton writes that the Mal Paharias "appear to be altogether unconnected with the Raj Mahal hill men". It appears that the natural surroundings of the Mal Paharia are mostly afforesting hills where the fear of the unknown and the unknowable, the denizen of forests and hills, streams and springs have crystallized their belief system, which in turn generates beliefs in various malevolent and benevolent spirits which are inseparable in their life. Under this backdrop the present **intensive study** is carried out among the Mal Paharia of Madhuvan village of Gopikandar block and for **controlled comparison of qualitative data** (to substantiate our data of intensive area of observation) the following villages had also been identified and studied, namely, Upar Murgathali, Gando and Asansol villages of Dumka block, Dumka district.

Table 3.1 : Block wise distribution of the Mal Paharia tribe of Dumka district

Block	Population		Total	No.of families	No.of Villages
	Male	Female			
1. Gopikandar*	2394	2318	4712	942	62
2. Jarmundi	1281	1231	2512	653	82
3. Kathikund	2030	2932	4932	783	67
4. Raneshwar	1088	1099	2187	550	39
5. Dumka*	1782	1034	3416	820	56
6. Jama	2039	1858	3897	803	86
7. Saraiyahat	546	556	1102	251	31
8. Masaliya	770	744	1514	350	44
9. Ramgarh	1567	1536	3103	687	70
10. Shikaripara	2115	2030	4145	86	73
Total	15612	15938	31550	6699	610

Source : Office of District Paharia Welfare Office, Dumka, Jharkhand, and January 2007

*- Study Area.

Field Investigation carried out in Madhuvan village of Gopikandar block and to substantiate our observation we have also collected data from Gando, upar Murgathali and Asansol villages of Dumka block which are very close to urban centres or within urban extended area of Dumka district.

There are altogether 34 major villages inhabited by Mal Paharia in Gopikandar block. Most of such villages are multiethnic. It is also told that there are number of Mal Paharia Gram Sabha in their block and in each such Gram Sabha there are again one to four neighbouring villages or hamlets of Mal Paharia depending upon size of villages and number of Mal Paharia families in the village. As per block record there are 34 Mal Paharia Gram Sabha consisting of 60 Mal Paharia *tola* (hamlet) or villages. The present investigation is carried out in Madhuvan village, which is in the north of Gopikandar block. The village Madhuvan is secluded on the hill slopes and in the midst of forest. In Dumka block there are 22 Mal Paharia Gram Sabha consisting of 56 Mal Paharia villages – most of such villages are multi ethnic in nature.

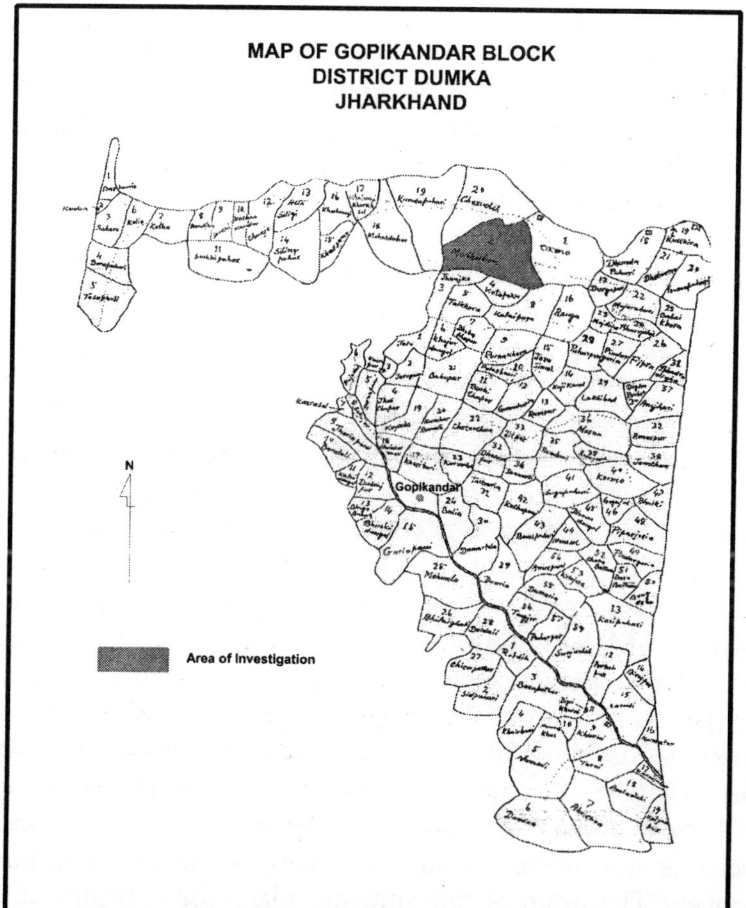

Village Madhuvan

The village Madhuvan is situated on the hill slopes and in the midst of forest in the northern side of Gopikandar block of Dumka district. Madhuvan is a multi ethnic village, dominated by Santal (66 families); followed by Mal Paharia (55 families), Ghatwar (12 families) and Maria or Lohar (2 families). Village headman is a Santal (named – Baburji Hembram). There is no Christian in this village but just on the foothill of this village – Durgapur and Ormo villages having Christian Santal families). The village Madhuvan is under Ormo Panchayat and in Ormo Panchayat there are 26 villages. The river Banshloi flows from north of the village foothills and it is usually a boundary line of Mal Paharia and Sauria Paharia settlement area with some overlapping. In fact all the ethnic groups are segregated from each other by forming tola or hamlets. This area is infected with Kalazar. The school *para* of Madhuvan village is lineally arranged among Mal Paharia *gotia* (minimal lineage) people while *nicher para* and *bayra dhangal para* are scattered and huts are dispersed from one another in various parts of hill slopes. The weekly *hat (*or, market day*)* locally known as *hatia* is held at Durgapur on Saturday and Gopikandar block headquarter on Wednesday and Sunday. Chiefly the village has two hamlets viz. *latar tola*, which is in the east, downwards while *upar* or *chitan tola* is in west. There is no electricity in the village. Roads are under construction under the **project of World Bank**. Some drainage work in the village is under construction, which is being constructed without proper survey work. The height of drain is higher in level than the discharge of water from each household. More so, the village is situated in the slope so naturally the water will flow down; therefore the expenditure incurred in this head is not worthy at all, it is simply misuse of public money. The drain is the breeding place for mosquito and flies because by depositing night soil (children use it as a place for defecation) the place becomes dirty. There is one grocer's shop, two Television sets (battery operated), four motor bikes possessed by Mal Paharia.There are one primary school (class I-V), total students 50 (of which male 23 and female 27 in number), and one high school and middle school are 7 km away at Durgapur village. For drinking water they depend on well which is far away from their residence and at the foot of hills. Though there is a tube well in front of the primary school but as usual it is not working and acute water crisis starts from April and continuing to June in every year. There are number of transistors in the village. During evening they assembled around transistor for listening news, songs etc. The nearest health center of the village is either at Gopikandar – 14 kms. away or at Amrapara – 15 kms. away on the north after crossing the Bansloi river. Amrapara is situated in Pakur district of Jharkhand.

Now in the following lines a demographic picture of the Madhuvan village is given in order to understand the socio-economic status.

Table 3.2 : Sex Ratio of Mal Paharia Age-group wise Village – Madhuvan, Total families- 56

Age group	*Male*	*Female*
0-10	62	67
11-20	38	30
21-30	20	27
31-40	24	24
41-50	13	8
51-60	4	4
61+	7	7
Total	168	167

It reveals that Sex-ratio (F/Mx100) is 99.40.

Table 3.3 : Age-group wise Literacy rate of the Mal Paharia Village – Madhuvan, Block – Gopikandar, Dsit.- Dumka

Age Group	Illiterate		Level of Literacy I-VII ((including Anganwadi) College Level				VIII – X Only can sign				XI – XII	
	M	F	M	F	M	F	M	F	M	F	M	F
0-10	36	40	26	27	-	-	-	-	-	-	-	-
11-20	6	7	26	17	5	6	1	-	-	-	-	-
21-30	11	19	1	2	2	3	4	1	1	0	1	2
31-40	11	18	5	2	3	0	3	1	-	-	2	3
41-50	6	8	2	0	1	0	2	0	-	-	2	0
51-60	3	2	-	-	0	0	0	0	0	0	1	2
61+	5	7	0	0	0	0	0	0	0	0	2	0
Total	78	101	60	48	11	9	10	2	1	0	8	7

Of the total population 53.43% are illiterate, 46.57% literate, and only 9.55%literates are having school final and higher secondary level education.

Table 3.4 : Family Type among the Mal Paharia Village-Madhuvan

Nature of Family	*Number of families*
Nuclear / with dependent	40 (71.43%)
Vertically extended	8 (14.29%)
Laterally extended	1 (1.78%)
Composite	1 (1.78%)
Broken	2 (3.58%)
Single Member domiciled	2 (3.58%)
Incomplete with dependent	1 (1.78%)
Incomplete	1 (1.78%)
Total	56

It appears from the above Table that nuclear family is mostly found among the MalPaharia.

Table 3.5: Family Size Among the Mal Paharia Village: Madhuvan

No. of individuals in a family	No. of Families
1	2
2	1
3	6
4	7
5	8
6	10
7	9
8	5
9	4
10	2
11	1
12	0
13	0
14	1

It appears from the above Table that the Family Size is 5.91 persons per family among the Mal Paharia of Madhuvan village, which indicates TFR (Total Fertility Rate) is high among them. As per National Family Health Survey (NFHS) record of Govt.of India the ideal type of TFR is 2.1 but it exceeds in Hindi belt while in North-east India it is within limit. It is also found that where literacy rate among women folk is high there TFR is within limit but differs and exceeds among the women folk of illitrrates or marginally literate.

Table 3.6 : Marital Status Age-Group wise among the Mal Paharia Village- Madhuvan

Age Group	Unmarried M	Unmarried F	Married M	Married F	Widow /Widower M	Widow /Widower F	Divorcee M	Divorcee F
0-10	62	67	-	-	-	-	-	-
11-20	36	23	2	7	-	-	-	-
21-30	2	0	8	26	-	1	-	-
31-40	-	-	24	22	-	2	-	-
41-50	-	-	13	6	-	2	-	-
51-60	-	-	4	2	-	2	-	-
61+	1	0	2	2	4	5	-	-
Total	101	90	63	65	4	12	-	-

The above Table reflects that there are 108 individuals in the reproductive age group, which indicates 32.23% are in this category out of total population 335.The sizable numbers are in unmarried category of which major in 0-10 age group, that is, 129(38.5%). It therefore can be said that population growth is harmonious.

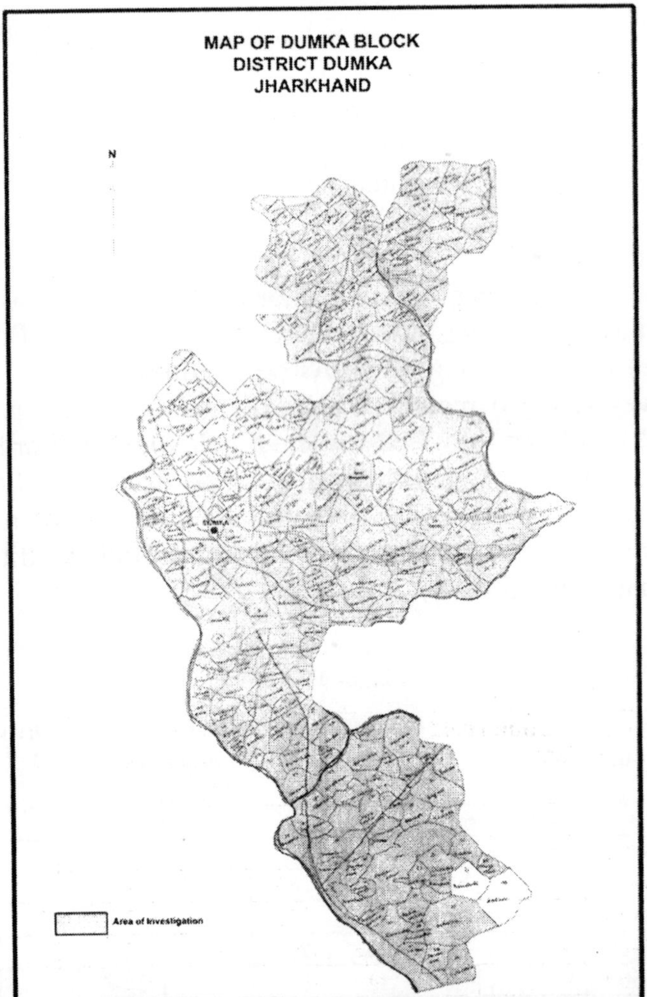

Other Studied Villages of Dumka Block

(a) Village **Upar Murgathali** is situated in Dumka block of Dumka Mufshil Police Station, Post office-Teliachawk, 12 km away from block office. The village is on the hilltop having a jeepable, all weather road. One side of the village is covered with thick forest. There are about 63 MalPaharia residential units and only 8(eight) Santal residential unit in the village. The village is having a health center, Public Distribution System, Primary Residential School. There are five hamlets, viz, *bagan tola* (20 MalPaharia residential units), *borbari tola* (8 Santal residential units), *Pahari tola* (15 Mal Paharia residential units), *Uparpara tola* (14 Mal Paharia residential units), *Nicherpara tola* (14 Mal Paharia residential units). There are about 36 Mal Paharia beneficiary families who received houses under **Birsa Abas Yogna**, cost involved for each house is around Rs. 56000/= while 3 Mal Paharia families received houses under the same scheme of Rs. 25000/= for each house. There is one Hanumanji *mandir*, all Mal Paharia actively participate on Ramnavami day, a *deheri* in the village, named, Madhusudan Singh, age-35, lives in *bagan tola* of the village officiates in this rituals. The Santals of the village are not participating in this ritual.

(b) Village **Gando** is 15 km. away from blockhead quarter-Dumka. It is a multi-ethnic village, dominated by Hindus. The communities inhabit the village are Kalal, Mirdha, Brahman, Ghatwar, Mehtar, and Mal Paharia and the village headman is from Mal Paharia community (named, Sibu Singh). It has following hamlets like, *niche para* (Kalal-10 families, Mirdha –22 families, Brahman-1 family, Ghatwar-2 families, Mehtar-1 family and Mal Paharia-22 families), *upar tola (Brahman*-1 family, Bania-35 families, Ansari-35 families, Bengal Naua-2 families), *mazdia gando tola* (Ghatwar-9 families), *badebathan tola*

(Ghatwar-16 families), *kurmatoli* (Ghatwar-8 families), *zapahari* (Ghatwar-6, Santal-6 and Mal Paharia-2 families). The weekly bazaar held on Wednesday and Sunday. There is one nationalized bank and electric facility in the village. The village is having a temple of Siva-Parbati. The idols of Kali, Durga and Sarawasti are worshipped regularly and the Mal Paharia participate in this ritual activities. The Gando village is considered as heritage village among the Mal Paharia because it was the headquarters of the chief of their estate (mentioned earlier in Chapter-2). Till date ruined and dilapidated estate's fort is visible.

(c) Village **Asansol** is 6 km away from block head quarter and almost adjacent to aerodrome of Dumka district. It is multi-ethnic village having Brahman, Santal, Koiri, Harijan, Khaira, Mal Paharia, Nai, Teli, Mirdha, Ghatwal, Goyala and others. The Mal Paharia are distributed in following *tolas* of the village, viz, *bagan para* (6 families), *pradhan tola* (20 families), *niche tola* (10 families), *bich tola* (8 families), and *sarak tola* (11 families) The village headman is a Mal Paharia (named Sibon Pujar, age 60).There is a Residential Paharia School for boys (Class.I-VI), co-ed Middle School (Class I-VIII), a Primary Health Centre, tube well and wells for drinking water but the village is devoid of electric facility. The Mal Paharia of this village identify themselves as 'Mal'. Under **Birsa Abas Yogna** eleven (11) families received houses in the year 2006 and six (6) families got it in 2007, while, under **Din Dayal Abas Yogna** nine (9) families got their respective houses in 2006.

4

Survival Strategy:In the Shadow of Ritual, Belief and Practices

Religion is regarded as one of the most important aspects of human society.It cannot be touched but felt in mind, that is, empathy. It is a covert phenomenon of human kind expressed through some acts and performances. Religion as a whole has a very broad spectrum. It has its structure consisted of several benevolent and malevolent deities and spirits and they are propitiated through some rituals and ceremonies. Each of which has functions expressed in the form of performances. Thus religion has both structure as well as function, which are well knitted.

Again religion has come out as per the necessity of human society. In fact, religion is the center or core of culture of a society. It guides the society in each and every sphere of life. A person is to abide by the norms of a society and definitely plays an important role to shape the culture of the society and to dictate the basic values.

To the authors' mind, **religion is a phenomenon of social articulation followed by ritual and practices and by practising it, one feels secured as well as gets a**

feeling of an in group social bondage, which differs from other. The intricate dependence on various benevolent and malevolent spirits, become the part and parcel of their survival strategy in a particular ecological niche.

Efforts have been made to examine how far the Mal Paharia cultural life is dependent on their beliefs on supernatural power and whether they are able to ignore their age-old tradition and belief system due to the influence of the outside world. Mal Paharia is one of the tribes who live in a geographically difficult area where they always have a feeling of insecurity and uncertainty.

Madhuvan is a village situated in the forest environment and again the Mal Paharia hamlets are situated in the denser portion of the forest at the higher altitude of the village. As they live in such a geographical background where they face an uncanny feeling of unseen spirits, that is, in an adverse situation, to get strength in mind, to combat with the mysterious events, they get hold of the supernatural power. Hence their life is very much influenced by the belief in supernatural power and by their propitiation of spirits, which holds an important position in their religious life.

Mal Paharia has their own priest or religious practitioner who is known as **Deohar** or **Pujar / Pujahar**. The post is hereditary. He has his assistant called **Fuljharia** and a messenger called as **Gorait** who informs and invites all Mal Paharias to attend and participate in the rituals and festivals. He also collects contributions from the villagers in case of any ritual and festival organized by the community or by the total village.

Beside they have an **Ojha / Ojha guru** -sorcerer of their own community who is consulted in crisis situation such as disease and death etc. To be an **Ojha** it is thought that one should have knowledge to detect and tackle the malevolent spirits and to neutralize their evil acts by suggesting the remedies. In addition to these, in most cases **Ojha** also acts as medicine man. If one **Ojha** fails to cure a person then they consult **Jan guru** – the sorcerer of the Santhal community who is believed to be more powerful than their own **Ojha.**

They have several sacred places meant for the ritual performances. They call those as **Than**. rituals. Some of these **Thans** in the studied villages are **Goriya Than**, **Jahar Than, Singh Bahani Than** (rider on a lion-one of the names of ten armed Durga), **Kali Than /** or **Chordanu Than, Chitipila Than**, **Kumhar Deo Than** and **Ormu Than.** In those **Thans** the worship of **Pahar thakur, Dharti, Bhui dev,** etc. is done. In Gando village, the situation observed is different. In the village, there are two temples. In one temple, there are idols of Kali, Durga, and Saraswati. In another temple Siva and Durga are worshipped. They participate in the puja collectively with other Hindu neighbours of the village.

Beside these temples there is a sacred place at Singh Bahani hills where during the regime of Gando Raja, they used to worship Singha Bahani, supposed to reside in a cave. In this village there is no separate *than* (alter) except the *keora than*. In this *than*, there is a *keora* tree, very thick trunk of *sakhoa* (*Shorea robusta*) tree and a bush of *keya* plant. There is a myth behind the establishment of the *than*. It is told that during the Hul (1855) Santals rebels killed the then Pahariay King of Gando. His name was Dig Vijay Singh. He was beheaded. His head was buried in that bush. This place is regarded as a very sacred place by the Pahariyas and on each and every occasion even in the life cycle rituals they visit the place with vermilion and turmeric to sanctify those out of touching on the burial ground prior to using in usual ritual. A pigeon or a cock is sacrificed in the name of the King. Deheri performs the ritual; women are not allowed to attend the ritual there.

In the village Murgathali, there are several *thans* of Durga, Lakshmi and Kali and very recently they have established a temple of Bajarangbali or Hanumanji. Ramnavami is performed where Mal Pahariya along with Santals and other Hindu communities of the village participate.

Asansol village is very close to Dumka town. In this village also the Mal Pahariya have their own *thans* attached to their homestead as well as in various locations of the village where they perform rituals and festivals together at the community level.

Except all these *thans*, each and every family has **Mara Morpa or Marha Morpa** – the place of their deceased ancestors. They establish those as the abode of the souls of the deceased ancestors after the performance of *sradh* ceremony. In fact in Madhuvan village they establish **Mara Morpa** in most of the cases by the side of the hearth. The *chulha* or hearth is regarded as very pure and auspicious to them. So they prefer to establish it there. In some cases it is established at a corner of the courtyard but the place should be very clean. Three vertical lines are drawn there with vermilion, which signify the place as symbol of **Mara Morpa.** They believe that their deceased ancestors are their guardian deities who are worshipped everyday and on every occasion, ritual and festival. They offer new crops to those ancestors prior to their own consumption. In case of any unnatural death, they do not place the soul in the place, such souls are regarded as malevolent spirit and they are driven out outside the boundary of the villa‿‿. Again within the boundary of the household, sometimes they establish their household deities also in the courtyard.

They have divided their worldly deities and spirits into two divisions – the **benevolent** (i.e. deos / devata / puja / ma / thakur) and the **malevolent (**i.e.jonkh /bhut**).** Among their **benevolent** deities the **Surja Devata** is the supreme authority. Everyday in ·ly morning they propitiate the deity. The families who have taken Sun God as a lineage God perform **Surjaho** – the elaborate festival of the Sun God after the interval of three to five years according to their custom.

Among other benevolent deities, **Pahar Thakur** (also enlisted among the malevolent spirits), **Dharti** or **Basumati Ma, Lit Mai**, **Lit Baba** (their originator), etc. along with their ancestors established at **Mara Morpa** are very important to them. They propitiate them through various rituals, which are mainly **connected with their economic life**. Some of those are **Maghi Parab or Akhan puja** performed to get protection from the snake, scorpion and other ferocious animals of the jungle, and when they go for collection (an important and compulsory occupation) in the deeper forest and also for a good harvest and protection of their cattle. They also worship **Mahadano, Chordanu** etc. spirits (those will be discussed later) for the protection of their crop. In each and every third year, just after **Maghi** puja, they perform **Bhui Dev** (mother deity-earth goddess) puja. They bring two *sakhoa* twigs and fit those in the courtyard of the **Pujahar**'s house. Upper portion of the twig is bifurcated and an earthen pot filled with *pochai* is placed upon the twigs, then they dance encircling the vessel and when they worship all the **Bhuts** (evil spirits) and **Deos** (the benevolent spirits) by uttering their names and salute them. During **Maghi Parab**, they also worship **Ghat Deo** – the deity at the boundary of the village, acts as the guard deity. In Madhuvan village his place is situated between Madhuvan and Ormu village. After performance of **Rohini Puja** they are allowed to take out seed for sowing otherwise the **Bhui Dev** will be displeased. They perform **Ashari Puja** collectively just prior to the start of monsoon cropping and also at family level, with a prayer to their deities and ancestors for bumper crop for each and every household. They sacrifice a he-goat as stated earlier and Mal Paharia males consume it in the village border. The blood of sacrificed goat is sprinkled at the border with a belief that they are driving out all the evils from the village and in this belief they set free two black pigeons symbolizing that they are driving out all the evils in the form of those two pigeons. These are done to protect the village from all types of evils and malevolent spirits who may attack from outside the village. In this ritual they offer all the new items of the season such as *chhati* (mushroom), new leafy vegetables, *phutka* or *kondki* – a potato like tuber etc. to their deities and ancestors of the family. Similarly in **Charak Puja**, when the mango seeds mature, they worship **Sing Bahani,** offer her the newly ripened fruit and only after this they eat this fruit. In the event of decline it is believed that tiger would enter into their village to make their life miserable.

All this can be described as ritual symbolism. Among the most revered symbols in Hinduism, two are quintessentially a part of its culture and representative of its general ethos. The first one is *aum / om,* the standard sign of Hinduism. It is often prefixed and suffixed to all Hindu *mantra*s (chants) and prayers. It contains an enormous and diverse amount of symbolism. Hindus consider its sound and vibration to be the divine representation of existence, encompassing all of manifold nature one eternal truth. While, the second symbol is *swastika*, a Vedic Arya or noble symbol. It stands for stability within the power of *Brahma* or, alternatively, of *Surya* (Sun). It is an equilateral cross, with arms bent at right angles, all turning in the same direction, usually clock-wise. But Indians also use the left-handed *Swastika* (normally assoiciated with esotrric Tantric practices) that rotates anti clock-wise. Its rotation in four directions at right angles has been used to represent many ideas, but primarily to describe the four directions and their harmonious roles. This symbols has been used in Hinduism since early Vedic culture and is still widespread in the Indian subcontinent (Raovallurupalli, 2009).

Thus, the ritual symbolism carries an altogether different meaning among the secluded tribal group. The representation of this symbol/sign carries a value-loaded belief system which is very much embeded with the core of sentiment under a particular culture which is flourished and nurtured in a particular geographical terrain. Therefore, various deities among the Mal Paharia apparently represented by some *than* (alter) or a piece of stone, i.e., a kind of animism, have a tremendous cognitive meaning at their cognisance level of mind. This cannot be removed until and unless interest in education is not created. Although, it is observed that with the practising of various rituals for their sustainable living they also practise conservation of their forest and agricultural produces and minor forest produces too. This aspect among the Mal Paharia is very much helpful for sustainable living in such hilly-forest terrain of Dumka. The propitiation and performances of various rituals by the Mal Paharia are chiefly for welfare purposes. These are as follows:

Makai Puja is another similar ritual performed at family level when the maize gets ripened in the cultivable land, gets ready for harvest. In this ritual, they offer five bunches of maize grain each to **Kali, Mahadeo**, **Lit Mai**, **Lit Baba** (their originator), at **Mara Morpa** with a prayer that they are offering the new crops to the deities and ancestors as a thanks giving ceremony, and seek their blessings. Then they are allowed to take the new crop with a request that they should not suffer from any kind of stomach problem, headache and other diseases out of consuming of those. They offer a pair of pigeons to **Kali Ma**, one red chicken to **Mahadeo**, black chicken to **Lit Baba**, **Lit Mai** and also to the ancestors at family level. Along with these items they offer five bunches of maize grain each to all of them with a prayer that they are offering the new crops to the deities and ancestors seeking their blessings so that they can produce produce enough crops in the year. After that they go to the *bari* land, offer puja there and cut the maize and bring those home. They then perform some rituals for purification of the harvested crop with a belief that if there is any evil eye on it, it will be driven out through the performance of those rituals. **Ghangra Puja** (a kind of bean) is performed at family level in the household and after that collectively at the **Singh Bahani Than**. This ritual is performed after *ghangra* – a variety of crop is fully matured, ready for cutting in the month of Aswin (September – October) Katick (October-November). This is a thank giving ceremony. They offer five bunches of maize grain each to all of the deities with a prayer to get their blessings for a good harvest and also to get protection from any kind of stomach problem, after consuming new crop and also to get protection from snakebite and other animals and insects, **Manasa Puja** is therefore performed to get protection from snake-bite and other poisonous creatures in their vicinity. They perform **Banashakti** (a malevolent spirit) **Puja** prior to the work of digging, locally known as *khobi* or *khonta*, for cultivation of *barbatti* or *ghangra* (a variety of beans) in their *vitto* land, with a prayer to protect them from scorpion, snake and other poisonous creatures during the time of cultivation. **Patjhari puja** is performed during the month Chaitra – the season *pat jhora* (transition period) that is, the falling of old leaves and appearence of new leaves. In the heap of the falling leaves, poisonous snakes and other insects may happen to hide themselves and would bite during cultivation in the hills. When the new leaves appear in some fruit bearing trees including mango, jackfruit, *mahua*, they perform **Bisho / Bisho Puja.** It is also performed at family level. After the ritual they take the new fruits; otherwise there is believed a chance of any type of mishap in the village; tiger and other ferocious animals may enter to kill them and their cattle. **Bahal Puja** is another ritual performed prior to the harvesting of paddy in the **Bahal Than** to drive out all the evil spirits from their surrounding area. Prior to the performance of the ritual if anybody harvests paddy, it is believed the death of the concern person or his family member is inevitable by the tiger.

They have several rituals associated with hunting. The period from April to June is regarded as their hunting season. They worship **Banashkti** (Durga) and **Pahar Thakur** (Lord Siva) prior to any hunting expedition.

Baski Nath Puja is performed during the time of **Makar Sankranti** and **Siva Ratri**. It is performed with a prayer for plenty of milk of the cattle. They pour water and milk at the root of a *bel* (wood apple) tree. They also perform rituals at their respective homes. In this way their economic life is very much oriented by their beliefs and rituals. All these rituals and ceremonies are performed for their overall protection from all dangers and hazards during their economic operations, to get success in life, for a good harvest, for the welfare of family and community seeking blessings from them.

To avoid natural calamities several ritual performances are in vogue in their society. In **Ormu Than** they worship **Dharti Ma** and during the ritual performance they speak the filthy language and abuse the evil spirits to the best possible length. They believe that when there was a great natural calamity known as *pralay,* **Dharti Ma** was disturbed by the evil spirits and was shaken heavily and to get rid of that turmoil several filthy and vulgar words were used to drive out the ghosts-spirits. Ultimately she was out of that crisis and became free from anxiety.

It is found that belief in supernatural power also has influences in their **life cycle**. They perform several rituals to appease their deities with a hope to get blessings from them. Again there are some ritual performances and taboos to get protection from all evil spirits. When a woman conceives, she is refrained from going to the forest and any water source alone especially during noon and evening;

with a belief that she would be attacked by malevolent spirit.

Childbirth takes in a temporary shelter constructed outside the house but within the boundary of the house. If the child birth takes place inside the main room, it is regarded as a serious offence to the ancestors established in the **Marha Morpa.** They are excommunicated and a heavy fine is imposed on them. The mother and the child are not allowed to enter the house till the performance of the purificatory rites as it is dishonour to their ancestors at Marha Morpa.

On the day of purification after taking bath, the woman goes to the tanks and other water sources of their hamlet with *sindur* (vermilion) and *kajal* (eyeliner). She draws three lines of *sindur* and two lines of *kajal* on the side/ bank of all the water sources to protect the water sources from all evils and impurity. Then she goes to each and every Mal Paharia household and draws similar lines on the pitchers and all other water pots, husking pedal, on the *okkhal /khonta/akhal* (digging stick) to safeguard the water sources, containers and other utensils and implements. On the occasion of *handipoda,* a ritual associated with a *bhoj* (grand feast) to all relatives and friends signifying total purification of the mother and the new born, performed in the third to fifth month and also on the occasion of *muhjhutti,* they offer cooked food to **Dharti Ma** and after that only *muhjhutti* for the child is performed with the consecrated food. With the performance of these rituals, the family is allowed to take part in all rituals and festivals.

The time suitable for **marriage** starts from the month of *Fagun* (February-March) after the performance of **Siva Ratri**-one of their very important ritual. According to them **Siva Ratri** is the celebration of marriage ceremony of **Lord Siva** and **Parvati** in the celestial world. So it is a very auspicious time to arrange their marriage in the terrestrial world.

In order to avoid crisis or danger in the family it is believed that prior to the marriage, *am biha* (marriage with a mango tree) for the bridegroom and *mahul biha* (marriage with a *mahua* tree) for the bride is performed. It is believed that if there is any danger including death for the couple after marriage, it will happen to the tree with whom the first marriage is done and in this way they neutralize the crises if there is any.

Just before the entry in the bride's village, at the entrance, the bridegroom's **Deheri** is given a red chicken, which he sacrifices at the boundary and the blood is sprinkled there. This is known as **Gaon Puja**. Through this ritual he drives out all the evil spirits and purifies the village. He in this way binds the village and obstructs all the evil spirits to enter and interfere in that auspicious occasion. The bridegroom's party crosses the boundary and enters in the village. After marriage when the newly married bridegroom and bride enter the bridegroom's village, to bind the village, similar ritual is performed. Then the couple enters the main room at the bridegroom's house, bows down the ancestors established in the **Marha Morpa** and all other deities established in and outside the room. Then the bride takes part in the cooking of food for the ancestors, lineage members, and other invitees. After the cooking is completed, the bride has to offer it to the ancestors at **Marha Morpa** and then she serves it to all the present there.

It is noted that the Mal Pahariya always avoid talking about death. **Death** as usual is considered to be a very sorrowful event. The Mal Paharia are always very suspicious in any case of death happened in their village. As a reason for death, at first they suspect that there may be some evil act of mischievous spirits or it might have been caused by some malevolent act of some person. The soul of a person died due to some accident or suicide or some epidemic disease, is not established in the **Marha Morpa.**

The other souls are established there and regarded as their guardian deities.

Annual Ritual Calendar

Sl. No.	*Name of the deity/ Spirit/Ritual*	*Month/ Date/ Time*	*Purpose*	*Type of deity/ Spirit*
1	Surjaho worship of Sungod	Between Fagun (Feb-– Mar) to Ashad (June – July)	Performed by the members of Surja lineage for the welfare of the lineage members	Benevolent
2.	Patjhari Puja – Deities/ Spirits – Banashakti, Kalgeriya, Pahar Thakur, Bhui Deo (Earth Goddess)	Chaitra (March – April) – the season of Patjhora, that is, the falling of old leaves	To protect them from any type of poisonous creatures hidden in the heap of fallen leaves specially the jungle where they go for collection	Benevolent and Malevolent
3.	Charak Puja Deity/ Spirit – Singh Bahani	In the month of Vaisakh (April-May)	Offerings of newly ripened mango, jackfruit etc. After that they can consume it. Otherwise tiger will come from jungle and kill them. Again they perform it to protect their houses from thunder	Benevolent
4.	Bisho/Bisho Puja Deities/ Spirits – Ancestors, Bhui Deo, Banashakti	Any Saturday or Tuesday of Vaisakh (April – May)	When new leaves come out in some fruit bearing trees and seasons products such as mango, jackfruit etc. even if not	Benevolent

Sl. No.	*Name of the deity/ Spirit/Ritual*	*Month/ Date/ Time*	*Purpose*	*Type of deity/ Spirit*
			ripened. After that they are allowed to take those. If this strict customary rule is broken, then there are chances of mishap in the village. Tiger and other ferocious animals may come out from the jungle and kill them and also their cattle.	
5.	Banashakti Puja	Vaishakh (April-May) Prior to the work of digging, locally known as *khobi* or *khonta* for cultivation of barbatti (a variety of bean)	To appease her and to keep her quiet. They worship her with a prayer to get protection from scorpion, snake bite etc. during cultivation.	Malevolent
6.	Rohini Puja Deity/ Spirit – Bhui Deo	Jaith (May - June)	After performance of the ritual, they are allowed to take out seed from their respective houses for sowing, otherwise Bhui Deo will be displeased	Benevolent
7.	Ashari Puja Deities / Spirits	Ashad (June – July)	Prior to the start of monsoon	Benevolent

Sl. No.	*Name of the deity/ Spirit/Ritual*	*Month/ Date/ Time*	*Purpose*	*Type of deity/ Spirit*
	– Ancestors, Bhui Deo		cropping the ritual is done with a prayer to the deities and ancestors for plenty of crops. In this ritual they offer new items, specially collected items of the season	
8.	Manasa Puja	Saon (July – August)	They worship snake deity Manasa seeking protection from snake bite and other poisonous creatures in their vicinity	Benevolent
9.	Chhed Puja Deity / Spirit – Singh Bahani (Ritual of sacrifice of *kohora* or Pumpkin	Aswin (September – October)	To show respect to Sing Bahani Devi who is equalized with Durga for the welfare of family and village and to get protection from snake bite, other animals and for welfare of the family and village	Benevolent
10.	Ghangra/ Makai Puja. Deity / Spirit- Sing Bahani, Kali, Mahadeo, Lit Baba, Lit ma, Ancestors	Aswin (September – October) to Katick (October – November)	To get blessings for a good harvest and to get protection from any kind of stomach problems after consuming new crop. The ritual is	Benevolent

Sl. No.	*Name of the deity/ Spirit/Ritual*	*Month/ Date/ Time*	*Purpose*	*Type of deity/ Spirit*
			performed to get protection from snakebite and other animals and creatures during harvesting.	
11.	Bahal Puja	Katick (October – November) to Aghan (November – December)	The ritual is performed prior to the harvesting of paddy in the *bahal than* situated in the forest. Evil spirits such as *kichling*, *dakin* etc. reside in and under the trees situated at the *than*(alter). They perform the ritual to drive out all those evil spirits at a safe distance from their village and surrounding areas. It is believed that prior to the performance of the ritual if anybody cuts even a bunch of paddy plant, he and his family will definitely attacked and killed by those evil spirits who will either come in form of tiger	Benevolent

Sl. No.	*Name of the deity/ Spirit/Ritual*	*Month/ Date/ Time*	*Purpose*	*Type of deity/ Spirit*
			or send a tiger from the jungle	
12.	Maghi Parab, Akhan Puja, Ghat Deo Puja. Deity / Spirit – Pahar Thakur, Dharti or Basumati Ma, Lit Mai, Lit Baba, Ancestors, Ghat Deo, Bhui Deo. Their cattles Goriya Devi, Chor danu, Mahadanu	Between the last day of Pus (December – January) to Fagun (February – March). On the day of Pus Sankranti they prepare sweet meat by new rice. Then on the first day of Magh customarily Maghi Parab starts. But it depends on the villager's ability and decision but it should be within the above-mentioned time span. On the third day of Maghi Parab they perform Akhan Puja	Welfare of the village and protection of their crops. To drive out all the evil spirits and at the same time to appease some of the malevolent deities. Ghat Deo is regarded as the protector of the village from all evils and stays at the ghat or boundary of the village to resist the evils from outside the village	Benevolent and Malevolent
13.	Baski Nath Puja Deities – Baski	Maker Sankranti	With a prayer for family welfare,	Benevolent

Sl. No.	*Name of the deity/ Spirit/Ritual*	*Month/ Date/ Time*	*Purpose*	*Type of deity/ Spirit*
	Nath (Lord Siva) and Dharti Ma (Durga)	and Sivaratri	plenty of milk of their cattle and prosperity.	
14.	Dharti Puja Deity / Spirit – Dharti Ma	Several times in a year	To avoid natural calamities, they perform rituals of Dharti Ma	Benevolent

Malevolent Spirits

It is worthy to mention that beside these benevolent deities, the Mal Paharia have a large number of malevolent spirits called as **jonkh** who have the mischievous power to do harm. Those roam in their vicinity always with a tendency to do harm for these people. They always have suspicious mind and are scared of those. In case of all types of disease and death, they blame evil spirits. Even if wind blows heavily or if there is incessant rain for a long, they blame the evil spirits. They lead their life with several restrictions, taken as protection from the evil act of those malevolent spirits. Some of the *jonkhs* are Rangadhari, Bisachandi, Kolkaowar, Kal Chaora, Kal Singh, Banashakti, Jalhari, Fulhari, Am Deo, Cham Deo, Goria Kali, Khunti Deo, Pat Bihar, Jonkh, Jokh Danu, Bhui Deo, Chordanu, Maha Danu, Singh Bahani, Patal Kali, Kiching, Smasan Kali, Maha Kali, Aghoriya Kali, Baghwas, Jora Jonkh, Karodanu, Mahul Baniya, Mal Jonkh, Kichling, Bel Kupia, Saonar, Bhowar, Pahar Thakur, Ichra Kudra Jonkh, Banashakti, Dalhar Jonkh, Swarga puriyatri Jonkh, Kalkumari Jonkh etc.

These *jonkhs* believed *to* be always having a tendency to do harm to the Mal Paharias. But when they are established at the *than*s at their own individual house they become the protecting deity for the family and their lineage. They are worshipped time-to-time in each and every occasion and rituals performed by the family and the lineage. Each and every family has one or two or even more Jonkhs of them. Even then they are worshipped very cautiously. In case of any mistake during puja, the spirit takes it as a very serious offence and cause maximum harm for the family. It is told that the villagers also worship the Jonkhs collectively in the ritual performances to appease them for their protection. Among the offerings sacrifice of animal, bird, egg and *ganja* are compulsory.

In the event of one's unnatural death, he becomes a *bhut.* The **jonkhs** are more dangerous than the *bhuts*. All the malevolent spirits together are referred as *masan.* Along with the worship of their deities known as **gosain**, they also worship these evils with a hope that those will not do harm to them.

The women who become *bhut* are known as *dakin, kichling* etc. Dakin roams through the cultivable land, by the side of river, hills etc. Those prefer to stay near water. Those always have a target to attack men. Dakins do not attack women; rather those are afraid of women. **Kichling** is more dangerous than *dakin.* Generally it does not go inside a person, but from outside it irritates a person who even sometimes becomes mad. As for example, *kichling* attacked once Buddha - a Mal Paharia male of Gando village. He became mad. He saw a buffalo and began to tell that it is his *devar* (husband's younger brother). **Kichling** also prefers to stay at waterside such as in pond etc. It wears white dress and plays musical instruments. They do not worship this evil spirit. To drive out **Kichling** in most of the cases, their *ojha* fails. So, they consult *janguru*(from Santal community) or *maulvi* of their locality.

Here a list of their **Jonkhs** with their activities is given below.

Name of the Jonkh with Activities

Name of the Jonkh	*Activities*
Pahar Thakur (a form of Lord Mahadeo)	According to the villagers Pahar Thakur is originally **Lord Mahadeo**. They worship him to get safeguard from ferocious animals and poisonous creatures during their hunting expedition. In each and every village, there is a Than of **Pahar Thakur**, represented by a stone placed under a *sal* tree. There is a *trisul* (trident) at right side of the deity. He is also worshipped in each and every occasion by family and at village level. At the rituals associated with cultivation, especially at the hills he is worshipped for bumper crop. During **Ashari** and **Maghi Parab**, they worship **Pahar Thakur** at village level. In this puja he is offered sundried rice, milk, sugar, liquor preferably of *mahua, batasa* and ganja. Ganja is one of the very important items among the offering. Not only in **Pahar Puja**, in most of their pujas, especially of the evil spirits, they offer ganja and in its absence tobacco leaves as one of the compulsory items of offerings.
Banashakti	– Among their **Jonkhs, Banashakti**-the wife of **Pahar Thakur** is worshipped prior to visit to jungle for hunting. Each and every hill has its own **Banashakti.** She is worshipped along with **Pahar Thakur**, whenever a person visits the jungle for hunting. She also protects the crops in the field. She is also worshipped during seed sowing both in hills and in their *bari* land. They dare to neglect her. If she becomes displeased, they will face various types troubles in cultivation and when they pass through jungle, it is sure that ferocious animals in the jungle will attack them.

Name of the Jonkh	*Activities*
Chordanu	Chordanu's primary duty is to protect the crops in the field, in the granary and other properties from stealing. **Chordanu** is worshipped both at family level and collectively by the Mal Paharias of the village. If any star falls from sky they are sure that there will be a theft very soon in the village at the direction where the star fell. Then **Chordanu** is immediately worshipped with a prayer asking for his protection from the theft. **Chordanu** is worshipped during any work attached with cultivation and in festivals of **Ashari** and **Maghi Parab**. **Chordanu's puja** is never performed inside the house but outside at the courtyard, in the **Chordanu Than** at the village and also in the hills. Women are also allowed to take the consecrated food except the pigeon offered to the spirit, which is cooked and consumed by the male there where the ritual is performed. If they do not perform the puja, then there will be less cereal production in the field and the spirit will do harm and as a result cereals and crops will be stolen.
Mahadanu	Another malevolent spirit or a form of **Lord Mahadeo**.His worship is done along with **Chordanu** to get bumper crop. His **Than** is present in the **Goriya Than**. A round stone represents it where they pour milk. The family can install it at the courtyard or *bari* land under a tree. During seed sowing and cutting he is worshipped. It also protects their cattle. If at night a jackal howls or an owl cries then they are sure that **Mahadanu** is displeased with them giving them warning of any type of mishap, accident and even death in the village. Then they immediately arrange for its worship with the sacrifices to keep him quiet by satisfying him.
Mal Jonkh	This *jonkh* stays at the *ghat* of Kurho Pahari hills. This spirit tempts the villagers who pass through the pathway of the hills, by keeping bell metal utensils, garland, silver coin etc. valuable items in the path. If by chance any villager feels greedy and takes the items at home, the **Mal Jonkh** follows him and

Name of the Jonkh	*Activities*
	enters his home and begins to stay there. As an impact of his entry in the home, family starts to face several types of disturbances and sickness within two or three days. Then they go to *ojha* to detect the cause and for remedies. They go to the *ojha* with a *sakhoa* leaf on which they keep mustard oil. The *ojha* rubs the oil on the leaf and tells the cause of the disturbances. He also tells how the spirit entered the house. The family then confesses what wrong they have done. Then the *ojha* worships the spirit with oil, vermilion, sundried rice, and a pot full with water, at the courtyard. He sprinkles water on the family head and other members of the family from the pot as significance that he is purifying the family. Then he worships **Mal Jonkh** at a corner of the room and establishes the spirit there. From then it is compulsory to worship the spirit once in a year as one of the deity of the family. The spirit is offered a white he-goat, rice, vermilion, puffed rice. The puja is officiated by the male head of the family. The family will consume the sacrificed meat. The family is liable to worship the spirit throughout the life. This spirit is also known as **Dhani Mal Jonkh**. He originally stays under a *simul* tree or a stream beside his original abode at the hills. He is also worshipped during harvesting time.
Tumba Jonkh	It roams in **Nandi Pahar** with a violin. He plays the violin at night roaming on the hills. He does no harm if he is worshipped during the cultivation of *barbatti.*
Dalhar Jonkh	This Jonkh stays in water sources such as in river, rivulet or stream, In the *khet* (cultivable land) prior to the harvesting, along with other deities and spirits he is worshiped during the month of *Aghan* (November-December). They worship it at a corner of the field. It is performed by the family head and women are tabooed to participate in the ritual.

Name of the Jonkh	*Activities*
Swargapur Yatri Jonkh	It comes on the males to kill him. The person attacked by this **Jonkh** gets seriously ill. Then the Ojha detects the cause of disease through his *tel patta* (mustard oil on *sakhoa* leaves) magic. The **Jonkh** is then worshipped with an offering of pigeon, red chicken and a he-goat. They worship the spirit to keep it quiet. Sometimes a stick is taken and beaten in the open air as if they are cutting the spirit into pieces. Sometimes the stick is touched on the body of the patient.
Baghowas	It resides in hills. Prior to the harvesting of *barbatti*, they worship the spirit with sacrifices of pigeon, chicken or he-goat. They believe that if they do not worship him, then he will bring tigers from jungle to their village.
Bhaman Jonkh	It lives in Karaleta hills and also roams in Konda and Tanter Pani hills. It scares people by taking different shapes and sizes in the form of shadow.
Yam Raja	It stays in Murga Pahari hills and is worshipped by villagers for safety in the hills when they work there. If it is displeased, death causes in the village
Karodanu Jonkh	This spirit is established beside **Kali Mata**. They worship him to keep him quite otherwise there would be illness in the village.
Rangadhari Baba	It is a very dangerous type of Jonkh. Generally villagers avoid it and maintain safe distance but when it enters a house, they are forced to establish it as a family deity and perform its puja. Then it becomes a deity of family welfare. He is established inside or at the backside of the house, worshipped at family level with the offerings of a red chicken. He is worshipped specially for the welfare of their children and family.

Name of the Jonkh	*Activities*
Ichra-Kudra Jonkh	This spirit is also worshipped at family level for the welfare of family during the month *Aghan* (November-December) at the side of a river or rivulet or under *peepal* or a baniyan tree.
Bel Kupia	He is another **Jonkh** worshipped at family level for the welfare of the family. He is worshipped after 14th January, that is, after the performance of **Makar Sankranti**. The consecrated food is taken by males and unmarried girls.
Saonr Bhonwar	This Jonkh takes the shape of a Bhonwar (wasp) and flies here and there. If they worship it, their property will be increased. Otherwise it will bite.
Bandro	When there is whirlwind, they think that Bandro is passing through the place. If anybody especially the children fall in that whirlwind, he or she becomes ill. The Ojha is called to drive out the *bhut* or the spirit.

They worship **Brahma, Vishnu, Shiva, Parvati, Manasa, Lakshmi, Saraswati, Ganga, Tulsi** (basil plant), **and Hanumanji along with Dharti Ma, Pahar Thakur, and Banashakti** etc. They worship them as per their own rules. No Brahman priest officiates the ritual. Mal Paharias in some Hindu dominated villages worship **Tulsi**. In many of their houses there is a **Tulsi Than** where they worship **Tulsi** daily in the morning and also in the evening. They pour water on the plant, light the lamp and offer flower and betel leaves to the deity. In this village there are persons who are confused whether **Tulsi** is God or Goddess. They pour water to get the blessings of the deity. A very few of them told that **Tulsi** was a very pious woman. Once her husband gone out without telling her. Tulsi was very unhappy started to meditate hoping her husband's return and ultimately her husband returned to her. This is a very important aspect, which gave **Tulsi** a very important status of Goddess. In her ritual *batasa*, *mihidana* etc. are offered during the morning time. After taking meat they are not allowed to perform her puja. Those who believe that Tulsi is goddess do not pour water on Tulsi on Sunday as it is told that on that day she gets menstruation. It is revealed from above that Hindu deity –Tulsi, become tribalised which is a kind of sankritisation.

But above all their religious beliefs and practices are enriched with the beliefs in spirits and most of which are malevolent.

They have belief in **Dayen/ Dain** (witch)**.** In case of any mishap or sickness they suspect that either any malevolent spirit or a **Dayen** is responsible for that. They cannot touch the spirit while suspect a woman as **Dayen** and torture her brutally even sometimes kill her only out of their suspicion.

These days a few Mal Paharia boys and girls have received higher education. They have daily contact with the block headquarters and even with Dumka proper. They have got opportunities to come in contact with different types of people with different religious beliefs, people with better technical knowledge and higher education with logical expression of various ideas and beliefs. In this situation these people have got a chance to exchange their ideas with them, got new ideas and they began to make an effort to give logical interpretation of their beliefs especially on the spirits and in most of the cases they failed to give satisfying interpretation. Again the Dayen or belief on witch and the horrifying torture on a suspected witch created a negative feeling on their society. Mal Paharia boys and girls often try to interpret these religious beliefs and the various sacred offices with a pragmatic approach. But institution of *kichling* or *dayen* has not been logically described to show their importance as shaman or sorceror, which is also a significant aspect of Mal Paharia culture.

Side by side they are influenced by the other religious beliefs and practices. Some have taken the membership of **Satsangh** of Sat Palji Maharaja of Hardwar and have taken *dikhsa* from Sattananda Swami. This Sangha has an ashram in Naihat of Dumka, 60 kms away from Dumka town from where some Mal Paharia families have also accepted *diksha*. They are the disciples of Sattananda Swami. He taught the Mal Paharia disciples to have a disciplined life with vegetarianism and abstinence from consuming liquor. They are told not to tell a lie and to wear white dress and to stop the traditional beliefs and practices, which are thought by the sect as superstitious.

Under the influence of Satsang some of them have stopped to keep **Mara Morpa** and **Thans** for different spirits and deities but they cannot deny contributing in rituals performed collectively by the Mal Paharia of the village and have not abstained from taking part in their traditional religious practices. Otherwise they will be excommunicated. They contribute half amount, as they do not take the consecrated food.

A few among them have been converted to Christians and belong to the Pentecostal group. Some of them have informed that they have been converted, as they are tired with the superstitious beliefs. Often personal harassment has led to conversion. The Christian Mal Paharias still take the help of *ojha* (shaman) to identify the diseases and to get rid of the malevolent spirits responsible for the diseases. If the *ojha* fail to cure the ailment and locate the *dain*, the Christian Mal Paharia stop taking the help of the *ojha*(shaman). There are instances that some of the Mal Paharias got converted on the issue of *dain*. [Case – Kalicharan Dehri (Age-63), a Mal Paharia, Bandajori, Dumka, Retd. Govt. Servant informed that in Jharkhand there are atleast 2000 Christians Mal Paharia of the Lutheran group of the protestant division. There are also some persons of the Pentecostal group. Kalicharan Dehri told that his parents and the family became Christian after they used to face several problems from their own people basing on their religious beliefs and practices. He informed once his elder sister became ill. They called *ojha* who after reading *telpatta (*oil putting on a *sakhoa* leaf) detected the evil spirit responsible for the disease. As per his advice they arranged for the puja of the spirit to appease it. They spent at least rupees five thousand in it. It was a very hard task to spend such an amount on those days. Even then after a few days his elder sister died. Then they stopped to attend and participate and perform their own rituals and festivals. In view of this the other Mal Paharia relatives and fiends were displeased. The Ojha was his father's elder brother. He through his magical performances detected Kalicharan's mother as a dain/dayen. He tried to kill her by throwing arrow. He convinced the other Mal Paharia of the village that she is a dain/dayen and it is necessary to kill her. The villagers attacked them and beaten them brutally. Then his mother decided to leave her own religion and to accept **Christianity**. They followed her and were converted as **Christian.** The other Mal Paharias became very angry with them. After the death of his father's elder brother his father attended the *sradh* ceremony where he was insulted. When he sat with others to take food he was told not to sit with other in the same line and was called later to take food but at that time the food was exhausted. In this way the other Mal Paharias insulted them. Interestingly, it is also informed by them that previously they were the priests, and in spite of their conversion to another religion, even today they are consulted in rituals and festivals. They give them the instruction and process of ritual but neither they attend the ritual nor take the consecrated food. Kalicharan told that though they have taken Christian religion even then they follow many aspects of their religion specially their life cycle rituals along with the performances of the Christian rituals.

The above discussion of the MalPaharia religious life depicts that as a result of contact with Hindus they have adopted some of the Hindu deities and their rituals in their own way again adjusting with the trtaditional culture. The influence of **Satsangh** and **Christianity** only has entered due to the negative impact of their beliefs and practices. They are trying to teach the people about the negative aspects of the Mal Paharia religion but not with much impact.

Therefore, the religious life of the Mal Paharia shows that Mal Paharia religion is full of beliefs on spirits, deities both malevolent and benevolent all of which have been evolved in their life to adjust with the uncertain ecological niche in which they live.

5

Survival Strategy: Economic Life

When religion is regarded as core of a culture, economic life may be compared to oxygen without which a society cannot survive. In discussion of economic life, one should always remember that economy of a society always grows as per the demand of local environment. A society living in hills and jungle has the economic life completely different with that of the society found in plains or in the desert. The locally available resources, on which the economic life stands, always differ in different geographical area.

The Malpaharia as already stated, live in hills and jungle. In olden days, there was thick jungle in their habitat. The Paharia had plenty of food in their locality. Hunting and collection of forest products were very important to them. After Government has taken jungle under their control as the property of the country, their right on the jungle products is restricted. Again as an impact of several developmental programmes and for several other reasons forest is gradually narrowed day by day. As a result their food storage of both hunt and collected items are not sufficient as it was earlier. Now a days hunting as an occupation has lost its charm. They hunt occasionally specially as an event of recreation and also in connection with certain rituals and festivals and in certain magic. In hunting they generally go in a group even, sometimes, taking members of other communities of the village. They hunt porcupine, hare, boar, birds, jungle cat, cock etc. Bow and arrow and different types of nets and traps are used. A very common type of trap is lumbhar funda, which is used to catch jungle cat and lumbha or hare. The members of the party as per their prescribed rules share the hunted items. If there is a big hunt by a Paharia hunting party of the village, then they arrange for a grand feast in their hamlet.

Collection - In spite of certain restrictions imposed on them, they believe that jungle is their own property. They enjoy the rights of collection of forest products collectively. There is no demarcation or bindings in collection from forest among them but when a tree grown in between the cultivable land of two different families, then the family takes the product of the tree whose field is closer to the tree. Jungle products till date have very important position in their economic life. It provides them their house building materials, such as wooden logs specially *rolabati* or *sakhoa* (sal) wood, bamboo, and grass, *roa* or palm leaves etc. Bamboo is also used to prepare various types of baskets, sup or winnowing fans, etc. items of daily use. Baskets prepared by this variety of bamboo is long lasting than the other variety.

They collect *sarai* grass used to prepare rope by which they tie logs and bamboo whenever needed in house making and canning of cot. The ordinary variety of grass is known as *kheir.* They collect bena grass to prepare ful *jharu.* (broom). They collect seeds and leaves of *benahata*—a local plant from jungle and sell those to the businessmen at local market at the rate of Rs.2/= per piece. Colour is extracted from those and used for various purposes. These have medicinal value also. Fuel wood, bamboo etc. are also collected from forest.

They collect several minor forest products such as sal leaves, bidi leave, sal twigs, various types of fruits, flowers, seed, leafy vegetables, mushroom, various types of tubers etc from jungle. They sell *murga chhati*- a variety of mushroom at the rate of Rs. 2/= per packet consisted of at least 10 to 15 pieces. Mahua flower is sold at the cost of Rs. 3/= for a *pai* or Rs.10/= per kg. One *tara* (20) of sakhoa leaves cost Re.1 to Rs.1½ They prepare dishes, and bowls etc. from sal leaves. They collect *kochera*- the mahua seed from which they extract oil for their use. S*akhoa* seed is consumed by them. They prepare charcoal by burning firewood and sell those at the local market- the weekly market from where they purchase vegetables, salt, oil, spices, soap, rice grain, pulses and kerosene etc. the daily needed commodities through the earning from those forest products. They earn Rs.200/= approximately in a month from the collection from jungle.

Table 5.1 : A list of their collected items is given below-

Season	***Collected items***
Garmi/Garam (Summer) End of February Ist.week of June	Leafy vegetables-kodra sag. Flower-mahua, sakhoa (sal), kachnar. Fruit-katkal (jackfruit), aam (mango), imli (tamarind), kendu (bidi), khejur (date palm) Jam, piyar, amsipra (guava) etc. Seeds-mahua, sakhoa.
Barish/Barsha (Rainy season) June-1st. week to October.	Leafy Vegetables-sola, kana, kundla, netia Fruits-sarifa. Other items- various types of mushroom such as- murga chhati, kamar chhati, agomas/ agowas, loa, parba, sugi, saranda, bansh chhati etc. Kondki-a potato like tuber locally called as abu or au, Various other types of au/abu such as chirkia, jaria, bhakta, mahua, tigo, chambo, jorwa, kosiyar, churka, foba, bharnari, boa, bokoya and etc. and young bamboo shoot.

Jara/Jare (Winter) October - February	Leaves and leafy vegetables- bidi pata, nakoa sag. Fruits- ber/kul, aola, behera, haritaki, kendu, bheloa, etc. Various types of au/abu as mentioned earlier grow during rainy season, ripen during December-January are eaten.

It is told that beside hunting and collection, they also undertake cultivation of both slash and burn and settled plough cultivation. Table of their occupational pursuits is given below.

Table 5.2 : Economic activities of the Mal Paharia

Sl. No.	*Types of Economic Pursuits*	*Male*	*Female*	*Total*
1.	Cultivation (M), collection and labour (S)	41	0	41
2.	Household work (M), Collection, cultivation, and labour (S)	0	73	73
3.	Cultivation (M), Household work (S)	16	0	16
4.	Household work (M), Collection and Anganbari work (S)	0	1	1
5.	Service only	1	0	
6.	Student	47	40	
7.	Financial agent of N.G.O.	1	0	1
8.	Household work	0	5	5
9.	Cattle herding	12	0	12
10.	Service at N.G.O. (M), Cultivation, Business (S)	3	0	3
11.	Household work (M), Collection, cultivation, Work at N.G.O. (S).	0	1	0
12.	Student (M), Helper in Cultivation/Household work (S)	0	3	3
13.	Cultivation (M,) Teacher, Social Work (S)	1	0	1

Sl. No.	*Types of Economic Pursuits*	*Male*	*Female*	*Total*
14.	Medicine man (M), Collection (S)	1	0	1
15.	Collection Only	2	0	2
16.	Masonry/Labour work	8	0	8
17.	Labour (M), Collection (S)	5	0	5
18.	Labour (M), Liquor preparation (S)	1	0	1
19.	Household work (M), Liquor preparation and sell (S)	0	1	1
20.	No Work	9	12	

* Persons below 5 years of age are not included in the table
M=main S=subsidiary

It is found from table that majority of the males; that is 58 males hold cultivation, as their primary occupation while in case of females cultivation is always the secondary occupation. There are three men also who have taken cultivation as secondary occupation beside their primary occupation of service under NGO. In case of women 81 are busy with their household work as their primary occupation. Cultivation, collection and labour are their secondary occupation. Though collection is a very important aspect in their economic life, but it hardly gets importance as primary occupation. The table shows that only two males are there who hold collection as their primary occupation. Whenever they go to jungle for some work, it is very common that they will do some collection. While collection as primary occupation is not enough to maintain a family. There are 4 Graduate males whose primary occupation is service under some NGO. There are some graduate males who work in Golden Trust Financial Insurance Company (GTFIC) as their agents who help the villagers to have policy in that company. One-woman works as Gram Sevika under NGO. Beside her primary occupation of household work, and other occupations as cultivation and collection, she devotes her time as an NGO worker and is very interested to do some developmental works for the society

A very remarkable feature comes out of the table that there are a large number of students; that is; 47 male and 40 female students among the Mal Paharia of Madhuvan village. Probably it is due to the inspiration provided to them by different Governmental and Non Governmental organizations who apprise them about the necessity of formal education in life. There is a Govt. primary school in each and every village. So it is easy for the villagers to send their children in school to educate their children and also for the mid day meal. There are some educated persons in Madhuvan who have established themselves in service, teaching works etc. There is an educated young person who works under NGO that deals with the cocoon of tasar silk thread. He became expert to examine the cocoons for which he has been given a microscope by the NGO named *Pradan* and is paid a very good amount of remuneration for his work. All these inspired the villagers to educate their children. There are two persons only whose primary occupation is collection. They are old and not able to do any hard work.

Now prior to the discussion of cultivation-their most important occupation, it is worthy to give a chart and some features of their different types of land.

Table : 5.3

Cultivable Land

Kheti (paddy field)				Vitto		Ghait (bari)
Bhadai/Burha	Badh	Sokra/Sokla	Bohal/Baihar	Pahari	Gharendi (Homestead Land)	Ghangra
(Varieties of paddy – Karhani, Sathi, Bhado, Jhingasal, Chaina etc.) Sowing – July Harvest-October 2. Varieties of vegetables such as brinjal, potato, tomato, onion, wheat, mustard, garlic, reddish etc. Sowing – Oct/Nov Cutting/plucking- - December	(bura dhan, bish maniya, mahipal etc.) 2. Varieties of vegetables such as brinjal, potato, tomato, onion, wheat, mustard, garlic, reddish etc. Sowing – Oct/Nov Cutting/plucking- December	(logha Sal, Kalam dhan, Sorna dhan etc.) 2. Varieties of vegetables such as brinjal, potato, tomato, onion, wheat, mustard, garlic, reddish etc. Sowing – Oct/Nov Cutting/plucking- December	(rajmahal, hajarpath, kistuchudi, putia, bohal, dudgdha kulma, bidlai etc. Baihardhan, 1010, 1036) 2. Khesari Pulse Sowing – Oct. Harvesting – Feb-March	1.Makai/Garandi,bajra /Janla, Arhar/ Lahar, Sutri/Kankro, ghangra, kudrum, bambaru, Muto, Kursa , kang etc. Sowing – June Harvest- Makai, ghangri: – August – Oct. Others – In Dec. 2. Kurthi/ – Single crop Sarguja Sowing – June Harvesting – Dec/Jan 3. Kodo – Sowing – June Harvesting – Nov. Or, 4. Til – Sowing – September Harvesting - January	(makai and ghangri with jhingi, bhindi, kundrum etc. vegetables) Wosing – June Harvest – Aug-Sept. to january 2. Sarso, mirchi muli, began, tomator October – Dec.	1st Year Ghangra Sowing – Aug. Harvesting – Dec-Jan. 2nd Year (The land is called as bari) Baro garandi (maize), arhar, bajra, surthi and ghangra Sowing – June Harvesting – December.

They have primarily three types of lands that are categorized according to their position. Those are again divided according to differences within them. Those are as follows:

Vitto / Bhitto land- It is again of two varieties- (a) Pahari Bhitto and (b) Gharendi Bhitto.

(a) **Pahari Bhitto** - It is situated at a very high position in the hills. They cultivate ghangra/barbate (a variety of legume), makai (maize), bajra, surthi, kudrdm, kosra, arhar, kurthi or sarguja, til, (all are varieties of cereals and pulses) in this type of land. They have to depend solely on rainwater for cultivation in this type of land.

(b) **Gharendi / Garendi Bhitto** - It is the land attached to their own houses which in other places commonly is known as *bari*. They also have *bari* but that is of a different variety. In *garendi* land also they cultivate ghangra, surthi, gehu (wheat), and makai with some vegetables such as jhingi, bhindi, kudrum etc. They also cultivate some Rabi crops such as-sorso and various types of vegetables such as mirchi, muli, began, tomato etc. This type of land is situated at a lower level where water retention capacity is more than the *pahari bhitto*.

2. **Ghait** or **Kurab**-This type of land is situated on the hill slopes locally called as *ghait* where during the first year, they cultivate barbate or ghangra also known as kawai. Next year in the same land they cultivate baro garendi or maize of bigger size, arhar, bajra, surthi, and also a little quantity of ghangra. During the second year the same land is called as *bari*. They cultivate in this type of land for two years. During the first year they solely cultivate Barbati by slash and burn cultivation, which is known as *kurao*

cultivation. During the first year they cut smaller plants, bushes and grass and keep those in the field for a few days till those get rotten. Then they dig a number of holes with *khonta* or digging stick at least of 2" to 2 ½" depth. They sow barbati seeds in those holes. They fell some big trees and keep those in the field as support for creeping during the growth of *barbati* plant. Barbati seeds are sown in July-August. It grows upto September. In October there will be inflorescence. During the festival of Durga Puja, they take a variety of legume and roam in the fair held for the festival to show it to a large number of people as they have a belief that the production depends on their ability to show the legume to more and more people. After that they keep those at the boundary of the *ghat* where they have cultivated.

During November-December they harvest *barbati.* Then they put fire in the land. The trees fell earlier in the previous cultivation are all burnt. The land has no plant but ashes, which act as manure. They cultivate garendi or makai, bajra or alna, sutri or kakro (a kind of pulse), kudram, bambaru, muto, metro/matro, kang. They plant *san* and *kushi* at boundary which act as hedge. They also plant varieties of sag or leafy vegetables such as jhinga sag, kadima sag, also which they also consume. This time the land is called as Bari land. All the items are sown during *ashar* (June-July) and except arhar all are harvested in *aswin* (September-October). Arhar is harvested in *aghan* (November-December). They eat *san* flower and *kushi* fruit. Kushi fruit is very poisonous. Prior to the preparation of *bhat* from *kushi* fruit, they wash it for at least five times. Then it is boiled repeatedly, they go to stream and place basketful boiled *kushi* fruits in the flow of running stream water and wait till it becomes sweet. It also has some medicinal values. In case of scorpion bite, it is broken and rubbed on a stone and applied at that particular cut or place of bite, the patient will generally get cured within one hour.

In the **Ghait**, a particular land meant for cultivation, they used to cultivate for successive two years. The land was then left as fallow land for next twenty years. Now, as the jungle is reducing day by day and as the plots are divided again and again resulting to smaller plots to accommodate all the Paharia families, they are unable to allow any fallow land for twenty years. Only after a gap of three to four or at the most six years they return to the same plot. If at that time too it becomes impossible for the owner to cultivate in that land, he may go to another person with a prayer to borrow a piece of land from him for two years. In lieu of that the original owner will get two bottles of liquor and a portion of the product cultivated in that land. This practice is known as *talmil*.

The third variety of land is known as **Khet**. The *khet* is again divided into four different varieties namely, *bhadai khet, badh, sorka* and *bohal khet*. The **Bhadai khet** is situated at the topmost height among the *khets* where they sow varieties of paddy during June-July and harvest during September-October. The next variety *khet*- the **Badh khet** is situated at a lower position, next to *bhadai khet*. Here also sowing is done in June-July and harvesting in October-November. The third variety of *khet*- the **Sokra khet** is situated at a lower position than the *badh khet* having a little more water retention capacity. In this type of land sowing is done in the month of July-August and harvested in the last week of November. The last variety of *khet* is **Bohal khet**. It has the capacity to store maximum water. It is situated at the lowest level where automatically watery. In this type of land also sowing is done in July-August which is harvested during December. Here they cultivate *kalipankaj* and *swarna*- varieties of paddy. Sarna can be cultivated in slightly high *sokra khet* as they can grow in slightly less water.

In all these four types of land, after harvesting of paddy, they produce several varieties of vegetables. In Bohal Khet they again sow khesari-a variety of pulse, which is sown in October and harvested in February-March.

Before seed sowing, ploughing, cutting and threshing at *khalihan* (threshing ground) they always worship Chordanu, Mahadanu/Mahadana with an offering of sweet, sugar, incense, and also red chicken for successful cultivation, and also for protection of their crop.

If a person has no land for cultivation, he can take a land on lease for two to three years from another person for a definite time period on lease. Generally the terms and conditions for lease is Rs. 500/= per 10 kathas of land for two to three years. This is called *satta* or *sattha bharna*.

When a person wishes to take a portion of land, in the jungle, for cultivation, which has no owner, he has to take permission from the village headman *-pradhan*. Generally he gives permission for two years. In lieu of that he has to give Rs. 500/= in cash, two to three handis of *pochai* (country liquor), a chicken, and at least 1½ kg. of rice grain for 10 kathas of land. Again he should give ½ *paili* of produced barbati in the first year and in the second year ½ *paili* of makai out of the total production to the *pradhan*.

They also have *adh batai* or share cropping system, which is locally known as *bhagị chash*. In this type of cultivation, one person has a piece of land where another person cultivates on the condition that he will render his labour in that field on the condition that the harvested crop will be shared equally. The person among the two who gives the seed locally known as bichon or bichhon, he will get separately the double measure of the seed given for cultivation. After that the two parties equally share the rest of the crop.

In some other informants view when a person works in another person's field, there is an agreement that the landowner will get 10 annas and the worker will get 6 annas of produce. This is known as *bhouli* in Hindi.

Sometimes they work in other's field. When they work in other's field in the village, they get Rs. 25/= to Rs. 30/= per day and when they work outside the village, they get Rs. 60/= per day as their charges.

When a Mal Paharia works in a field of a person of their own community, he does not get any labour charge. In lieu of his labour he gets similar service from the person in whose land he worked.

They prefer to add *gobor khad* (cow dung fertilizer) to their field and spray *bis tel* (a kind of insecticide) either by machine taken from mahajan or simply by broom. They have learnt about the insecticide from the radio.

There are several other occupations as depicted in the table. Interestingly it is seen that there are persons involved in several types of works under different Non-Government Organizations who run several developmental projects in the village. Among those NGOs the first name to mention is of AAA or Agrarian Assistance Association. They are working for the last ten years in Dumka district of Santhals Parganas among the tribal groups of this area. They are providing training especially in connection with agricultural works. They have constructed several women's organizations through which they are propagating various types of messages on cultivation, development of fallow land, protection of jungle, child care, children's education, etc. The women's organization has to control over the production, distribution and storage of the produced/ harvested surplus crops for future need.

This organization works for the development of fallow land and the protection of forest for which they have taken up Madhuvan and Gando village (i.e. studied village) and other 100 villages (approx.), which brought Indira Priyadarshini Brikshamitra award for the NGO - AAA in 1994 from the Department of Paryavaran, Delhi.

The Mahila Gramsabha of Madhuvan village has an Adhyaksha or President, a Secretary or Sachib, an accountant or Koshadhaksha. All of them were elected. It is told that if they can do some excellent work, then there will be no further election.

Women from each and every Pahariya family of the village are members of this organization. This organization again comes under a cluster in charge under whom there are several such organizations of other villages. Again, six cluster in-charges come under the Project Coordinator. This organization primarily deals with various types of works for development and to solve problems arise as hindrance for developmental works.

The Mahila Gram Sabha calls a meeting in each and every week where they discuss several problems of the village, education of their children, equal labour wage for both the sexes, protection of jungle, plantation of various fruit giving and economically very important plants producing cash crops such as mango, jackfruit, ashan, bair, sakhoa, sidha, etc. The trees such sidha, sakhoa, asan, bair are important not only for their fruits and wood but these are also suitable for cultivation on silk cocoon. They advise the villagers not to take loan from the Mahajans who lend money at the high rate of interest such as 15% yearly. This Samity also lends money at the rate of 10% yearly. As a result the villagers now a days have stopped to borrow from Mahajans except in cases of emergency.

Initially the villagers used to sell the collected forest products to the Mahajans at a cheaper rate such as Re.1/= for two *taras* or 40 bidi leaves. AAA. took initiative to purchase those at the rate of Rs. 2/= to Rs. 2.50/= for that.

The Mahila Gram Sabha lent Rs. 1000/= to each and every Paharia family as capital at an interest of 10% yearly repayable at three instalments. They also give loans to the villagers during their disease and crises. Fifty kg. of rice is given to the person suffering from Phylaria, Tuberculosis, Kalajwar, Malaria etc. and arranged necessary treatments. Those who are very poor and are not having hut to live in they are given loans even to the extent Rs.1000/= for house building at 10% interest.

The Mahila Gram Sabha strictly takes actions against *gutikarma* (in Santhali language) or *balmajdur*- engagement of child labour. In such cases they immediately stop the practice and send the child to school providing some economic assistance to the family. They help the old, widows and distressed persons. They help the old by taking initiative to pay Briddha pension from the State Government. They also help the villagers to have the card of Gramin Rojgar Yoyona by which the Government ensures one compulsorily 100 days labour yearly to all members of each and every family.

The Gram Sabha also helps the villagers by giving seeds on loan, supplied by AAA. After harvest the person who has taken loan has to return 11 kg. for each and every 10 kg. of seeds. Whereas the Mahajans take 20 kg. for each 10 kg. of seed. The Mahila Gram Sabha stores the returned seed and they have constructed a *bij gola* (storage of seed). Except this from each and every household, after harvesting of crop, the Mahila Gram Sabha compulsorily takes 10 to 20 *pai* of harvest to store in *anaj gola*. During lean period and in period of crisis the villagers get *anaj* from that *gola* for their consumption and after harvesting of crop they have to return the same quantity they had taken.

Last year the organization distributed the seed of Madrasi *ol* (a kind of tuber of South Indian variety). They were able to produce 10 kg. to 12 kg.-sized *ol*. The seed is again returned to the organization.

They are instructed to use traditional varieties of seeds. The women members visit door to door and collect traditional seed from the villagers. They also collect herbal medicines and preserve those.

The Mahila Gram Sabha arranges training to prepare and use organic manure and insecticides instead of using the chemical fertilizers. They are taught that chemical manures and pesticides are harmful for soil. Due to the use of those the land loses it's fertility, it becomes hard, water storing capacity is lesen day by day. Not only for the soil but also harmful for them as poisons of chemicals are accumulated in leaves, fruits, flowers etc. of those plants which are ultimately consumed by them.

They instruct to prepare *kechua khad* or wormi compose. They accumulate cowdung and leave earthworm in it and ultimately it becomes manure. Mal Paharias call it *ishar khad.* They also prepare compose *khad* with the help of leaves and cowdung deposited in a 3 feet deep pit. When it is completely filled up, it is closed by mud and left those for at least one month. By this time it gets rotten. At the time of cultivation, it is taken out and added to the soil. Another very important manure is named as *matka khad.* It is prepared in a *matka* or big earthen pot. At first half of the vessel is filled up with cowdung and the rest half is filled up with cow urine, water and ½ Kg. of molasses. Then the earthen pot is closed for six days. On the seventh day the lid is opened and the entire substance is stirred following addition of adequate quantity of water. Then it is applied to the cultivable land.

The AAA also trains them the way of preparing organic food and insecticides. The *neem*, *karanj* and *akowan* leaves are accumulated in a vessel made of mud, thereby empty portion of the vessel is filled with cow's urine and little water then the vessel is made air tight with the lid. After six or seven days they open the vessel and extract the decomposed leaves. Then they sprinkle the so prepared acquous insecticide on the plants specially affected by insects.

The Mahila Gram Sabha instructs them to produce Rabi crop, such as wheat, beans, tisi, peas, and khesari etc. which are sown in December and harvested in March. Among vegetables, potato, brinjal (egg plant), tomato, chilli, cabbage, cauliflower etc. are produced. They discard high yielding variety of seed, which is known as terminator seed as during cultivation they have to add chemical fertilizer to it. Instead of terminator seed they are suggested to use '*parampara*' seed as and in most of the cases they began to use this variety of seed. They successfully collected at least 75 types of '*parampara*' seed, through Mahila Gram Sabha which are distributed among the cultivators. In this variety no chemical fertilizer is used. They are of opinion that this type of seed can be used continuously for a long duration without adding chemical fertilizer in it.

Previously they used to sow a number of seeds of at least 5 to 6 in the same pit of the cultivable land. AAA through Mahila Gram Sabha taught them to sow a single seed in a single pit. They established that in such cases single plant comes out from a pit gets total nutrients from that pit without sharing with others. This becomes healthy and gives bumper crop of better quality.

There are other two organizations. Among those 'Pradan' or Participatory Rural Development Agency- an NGO primarily deals with the cultivation of tasar silk cocoon. Many of the young males of this village are involved in this project. They cultivate cocoon, and is sold in its mature stage to the organization. The organization time to time gives them financial assistance for cultivation. A person of the village is given a microscope by the NGO to ascertain the qualities of the cocoons for which necessary trainings were given to him by the organization. It is told by them that they cultivate tasar guti in asan, sakua, bair, haut, and sidha plants. Titli- locally known as *pokhia* or moths come out of the cocoon is of two varieties. The smaller sized *titli* is *nar* (male) *titli*; locally known as *joan* or *tira* and the larger sized *titli* is female one. After they come out, they become for union. At about 4 P.M. the cultivator drives out the male one and catches the female and keeps it in a leaf for eight days. It is kept in such a place where there is no chance of smoke. On the eighth day the female is freed. In the mean time it lays eggs. On the ninth day larvas come out of the eggs and those are distributed on *asan* tree and covered by net for six to seven days. Then the net is removed. By this time the cocoon is matured and they change their skin four times. After sixteen days the cocoons are fully matured to *tasar guti*. Those are then sold to the market. According to the quality the cost of the cocoon is fixed. Previously they used to sell the cocoons to the mahajans at a very cheaper rate. They ultimately started getting a profit of lucrative amount by selling those at a very high rate. 'Pradan' was trying to stop this practice. At present the cultivators sell those to Pradan instead of going to the mahajans. 'Pradan' pays Rs.800/= for the smaller variety and Rs.1200/= for the larger variety of 1 *kahan* that is; 16 *pan* of cocoon. A *pan* is consisted of 80 cocoons, so 1 *kahan* is 1280 cocoon.

Atma is another organization run by the State Government. It deals with several developmental works runned by the State Government. There are several projects run by the Governmental agencies. Work of road construction is going on in the studied villages Madhuvan and many other Pahariya inhabited villages. The expenditure is incurred from the loan of the World Bank. The labourers for that work in most of the cases are employed from that particular village and the wage for that work is Rs. 70/= per day irrespective of sex. In the studied villages buildings are constructed for them under the schemes of Indira Vikash Yojna and Birsa Abash Yojna.

It is observed that the Mal Paharia of the studied villages is changing their attitude towards their economic life. In Madhuvan they have got inspirations in cultivation as per the instructions of the NGOs. As they understand that those are profitable and also not at all harmful. It leads them towards an economic stability. They are now less dependent on the mahajans. They understand the necessity of education in life. There are a number of educated Mal

Paharia who are well established in service under Government and Private sectors, which are worth mentioning inspiration in their life.

8

Social Life and Kinship

Household is a residential unit within which production, child rearing etc. take place. In some societies household comprise families. There are instances that a number of members of the household are not in any way related to the head of the unit. For example, in Africa especially in Nigeria the households of the Kings and Chiefs are comprised of individuals who are not in anyway related to the king or the chief.

Household is the basic unit for production and consumption, which revolves around *chulha* (hearth). During field investigation in various Mal Paharia villages of Dumka district it is observed that the customary unit of the Mal Paharia is household or *paribar* and through which the number of population at a site or village is expressed. Contextually *chulha* means a group of individuals who produce from same *vitto* and *kheti* land, consume and live together and also share a common shelter under one roof with a common *chulha* or hearth.

In Madhuvan village, there are altogether 56 Mal Paharia households in three hamlets of the village, viz, *school para, nicher para* or *besga para* and *bayra dhangal para*. It appears from the empirical data (vide **Table 3.3**) that the family type among the Mal Paharia of Madhuvan village is, majority of the families i.e. 40 (71.43%) are of nuclear type; that is, composed of husband, wife and unmarried children and sometimes also with dependents like, father or mother or the both.

The average family size among the Mal Paharia of the studied Madhuvan village is 5.91 persons (vide **Table 3.4**). The basis of kin grouping (*saga-samandhi / kutumb*) is traced either genealogically or through marriage. Although clan or *gotra* is absent among them. The minimal lineage group that is maximum upto third ascending generation are considered as *saga* exogamy. Cross-cousin marriage is not allowed and the extension of close kin group is carried only upto third ascending generation of both father's and mother's side. Though there are number of titles among the Mal Paharia, and there exist hereditary distinctions. The titles are – **Deheri** (involved in worship activities), **Grihi** (cultivator), **Pujar** (worship/ritual activities), **Ahiri** (specialized in hunting activities), **Rai** (adviser), **Manjhi** (village headman), **Singha / Singh** (title of their raja was traced from **Singha / Singh** – a warrior group like Rajput), **Dalai, Laiya, Kunwar, Paharias, Patar** and **Sardar**. But there is no hierarchy among these titles. The titles are not exogamous. Intramarriage and intermarriage between the titles is permitted. Moreover, a **Deheri** marrying a **Deheri** or a **Manjhi** marrying a **Manjhi** etc. is also permitted. In each and every household among the Mal Paharia there is a seat close to *chulha,* of **Mara-Morpa** (ancestral household deity), which is very sacred one. It is believed that the ancestral spirits of the Mal Paharia are thought to be moving with them and render help at times of crisis.

The kinship terminologies used by the Mal Paharia for different kin members clearly suggest that the terminological system of tribal people is denotative and according to Mukherjee (1981) the tribes living in Gujarat, Uttar Pradesh and Bihar (undivided) tend to have **denotative system** and particularly Bihar is strongly denotative. As per Lowie's classification it is **bifurcate collateral,** that is, they used separate term for Father as **Buba**, Father's brother as **Jetho/Kaka** and Mother's brother as **Mama**, while according to Murdock's classification their kinship terminology is **Hawaiian type** i.e. all cross and parallel cousins are called by same term. But in all cases descent in patrilineal. It is also reported that predominant typologies to which majority of the Indian tribes conform are **Iroquois** and **Hawaiian** which have spread all over India except Nagaland of North-East India (Mukherjee, 1981).

The kinship terminologies among the Mal Paharia are as follows: -

Table 6.1 : Kinship Terminologies among the Mal Paharia

Sl. No.	*Kin term*	*Term Address*
1	Fa Fa	Dada, Bara Buba
2	Fa	Buba
3	Mo Mo	Didi
4.	Mo	Mai
5	Fa Mo	Bado Mai
6	Mo Fa	Bado Buba
7	Fa Br (el) Fa Br (yo)	Jetho Kaka
8.	Fa Si	Pisi(yo), Putiyai or Phua or Nana(el)
9	Mo Br	Mama
10	Mo Si (el) (yo)	Jethiai Masi
11	Br	Dada (el), By name (yo)
12	Si	Didi (el), by name (yo), Chota beti (yo)
13	Fa Br Da	Didi (el), Bahin(yo)
14	Fa Br So	Dada (el), Bhai (yo)
15	Mo Br Da	Didi (el), Bahin (yo)
16	Mo Br So	Dada (el), Bhai (yo)

17	So	Beta
18	Da	Beti
19	So So	Nati
20	So Da	Natin
21	Da So	Nati
22	Da Da	Natni
23	Dau Hu	Jowai so
24	So wi	Bahu so
25	Son's Wi Fa	Samandhi
26	Son's Wi Mo	Samandhin
27	Dau Hu Fa	Samandhi
28	Da Hu Mo	Samandhin
29	Hu Fa	Buba so
30	Hu Mo	Mai so
31	Wi fa	Buba so
32	Wi Mo	Mai so
33	Step father	Buba or kaka

Life cycle Rituals-

When a woman is in her monthly cycle, she is not allowed to sit on a cot as she is regarded as polluted. She is not even allowed to cook for the family till she is purified by taking purificatory bath after completion of the monthly cycle.

Birth

During pregnancy, a woman is restricted to go to the forest and any water source alone specially during noon and evening, as they believe that there are several types of *jonkhs* in their vicinity who through their mischievous / malevolent acts harm to the woman.

Delivery takes place outside the room at a corner within the courtyard behind the main room. A temporary shelter is constructed for the purpose, which is known as *chuto*.

If childbirth takes place inside the room, it is taken as a serious offence to the ancestors at *marha morpa*. So they construct a separate shelter for delivery. A midwife locally known as *domin* of his or her own ethnic group assists the pregnant woman. Previously the domin used to cut the umbilical cord by an arrow now it is replaced by blade or a *hansua*. It is buried at a corner of the courtyard. If the child is a male then the *domin* gets Rs. 10/= to Rs.15= as her remuneration and for a female child the remuneration is less. In the *chuto* the woman continues to stay with her newborn baby and husband till the completion of pollution period. The pollution period lasts for 12 to 15 days. On that day the *lapit/naua* (barber) is called who pares the nails of the parents and shaves the beard and head of the father. He touches his implements to the baby. Then the father breaks the *chuto* and throws all the materials used to construct the *chuto* and the materials used during the pollution period in the jungle. Then purificatory bath is taken. After that they enter the living room. If the childbirth takes place inside the main room, it is regarded as a serious offence to the ancestors established in the *marha morpa*. They are excommunicated and a heavy fine is imposed on them, which includes at least 20 *pai* of rice and one *handi* of *pochai* to be given to the community members. The thatch is completely broken and again arrange for new construction.

After seventeen days following the stoppage of bleeding, again the *lapit* comes and pares the nails. The mother and the child are bathed and then the woman goes to the ponds and other water sources of their hamlet with vermilion and kajal. She draws three lines of sindur and two lines of kajal on the side/ bank of all the water sources. Then she goes to each and every Mal Paharia household and draws similar lines on the pitchers and all other water pots, husking pedal, on the *okkhal / khonta / akhal* (digging stick). After taking purificatory bath the mother is allowed to enter the room but allowed to cook after performance of *handipoda*, which is performed after three to five month. It is a ritual associated with a *bhoj* (grand feast). On that day the naming ceremony and *muhjhuti* (first rice feeding ceremony) of the child are also performed. The date for *handipoda* is not fixed. It depends on how early can be arrangd the money for the purpose. Generally within six months it is performed. The family gives the Mal Paharia of the village, other invitees and friends a grand feast. All the Mal Paharia cognates undertake shavings and nails are pared by the *lapit* who is given Rs. 10/= to Rs. 15/= as his remuneration. The uncle or the maternal uncle of the baby sacrifices a chicken and it is also cooked. He performs *muhjhutti* ceremony of the child by touching *bhat* and the sacrificed meat for seven times on the mouth of the baby. The father can do this if there is no uncle. The father offers a portion of that cooked food to the *dharti ma*. With this *chhut* (pollution period) is overcome by the family. Then the father with him and all the invitees take the food. After performance of *handipoda* the family is allowed to take part in all rituals and festivals. The woman starts her daily routine of cooking. Till the performance of *handipoda* the child is not included in Mal Paharia society. The *deheri* (priest) is paid his remuneration both in cash and kind for his service. On that day they call at least two to three male members of the hamlet. A feast is given to the invitees and friends. If there is no other person in the family to cook then the woman after taking purificatory bath starts to cook for the family. In that case they offer one or two *pai* of rice grain and one handi of *pochai* to the *deheri* and in this way they become pollution free. She can bring water and can cook, but the child will be included in their society only after the ceremonial feast given to the members of the society.

Marriage

The Mal Paharia are an endogamous group of people hold lineage exogamy as their marriage rule where they avoid minimal lineage group, that is upto three ascending generations (which they can remember) of both father and mother's side. They call it as *dalpat sampark* (relationship like branches and leaves of a tree). At present they also consult *jamabandi* (land record) to arrange marriage, which is very authentic to trace the relationship. Child marriage was the rule but now age of marriage is increased. Traditionally marriage between *gotia* (consanguine) people was forbidden but the rule is now relaxed. It is already mentioned that there are three types of Paharia-The Sauria, Kumbharbhag and the Mal Paharia. All of these three groups are endogamous but the Mal Paharia have no objection to marry from the Kumbharbhag Paharia and vice versa. But they are strictly prohibited to marry the Sauria Paharia group, as they are beefeaters. Traditionally they are not allowed to marry within the village but have no restriction to arrange marriage with a person having same household deity.

There are several types of marriage among them. Biha or *sitthu /sirthu biha* or marriage by negotiation is the most preferred type of marriage. Love marriage or *bhulani biha* is also allowed if the marriage rules are strictly followed. Otherwise the couple is excommunicated and after paying compensations they are accepted by the society. Other types of marriages are marriage by exchange or *gaibadli biha*, by service or *munish biha,* marriage by force or *sindur dile,* marriage by intrusion or *ghar poshao/puisho/kudbi biha*, marriage by elopement *poyai/pnui, chhutbi biha* or remarriage. Sindurdan (putting vermilion on the forehead) is the most important ritual of marriage. In case of marriage by intrusion the girl enters the boys house with a *datan* (twig used as toothbrush, and two sal leaves. There is no expenditure in this type of marriage. To cut short the expenditure after finalization of marriage the guardians instruct the girl to do it. In *chhutbi biha* that is remarriage, the bridegroom dose not put sindur on the bride's forehead and in the hair parting. Instead of him, a woman performs the ritual.

The time suitable for marriage starts from the month of Fagun (February-March) after the performance of Siva Ratri-one of their very important ritual. According to them Siva Ratri is the marriage ceremony of Lord Siva and Parvati in the celestial world. So it is a very auspicious time to arrange their marriage in the terrestrial world. The period lasts till the rain comes. During this period they have harvest *anaj* (crops and cereals). Again from the month of Ashar (June-July) till the month Poush (December-January) they become very busy in their field having less time for relaxation. They arrange marriage and the stored *anaj* is also lessened. They are prohibited to arrange marriage on Thursday, Saturday and Sunday. They even do not start negotiation of marriage on these days. Both the parties are not allowed to visit each other's place on those days. Previously they used to practise child marriage. At present it is raised to15 to 22 years for a girl and for a boy even upto 25 years of age.

The proposal of marriage comes from the boy's side through a mediator locally known as *bortoyar* or *sirthu / sitthu*. Female mediators are known as *sirthian / sitthian* who generally belongs to their own community. If the girl's party has no objection then the boy's party along with sirthu proceeds to the girl's house. The boy can accompany the party. When they proceed to negotiate a match, if a crow caws or an owl hoots during daytime, which are considered as very bad omens, they stop immediately at least for the day and postpone it further for an auspicious day. On the other hand if a person is seen carrying a pitcher filled with water, they become very glad as it is considered as a very good omen.

The first visit is preferably done on the day of *hatia* (weekly market day) as arrangement of food and drink is easier on that day. When the proposed girl comes they pay her some money. This is known, as *kaniya dekha / mukh dekhni.* Exchange of liquor bottle between the two parties is customary. Both the parties except the boy and the girl drink the liquor. If the boy's party is not satisfied with the girl and not chosen, then the *sirthu* is given only a bottle of liquor as his remuneration. If she is chosen then the *sirthu* also gets a dhoti or a sari. The boy and the girl are individually asked whether they have any objection in this match or not. If both of them agree, the guardians proceed further. Next the girl's party pay return visit to the boy's house. The girl may accompany the party. This is known as *ghar dekha*. They come with some gifts consisting of garments (pant, shirt) for the boy. The girl's mother massages mustard oil on the boy's face, hands, and legs. She combs his hair and blesses him giving the presents and putting *dhan* (paddy grain) and *dubba* (a kind of grass, regarded as very sacred, used in all auspicious events) on his head. After that the boy's party gives a feast. After that the girl sometimes continue to stay there with the boy as his wife and children are also born. This is known as *chumna biha*. In this type of marriage, no bride price is given and to cut short the expenditure, sometimes this type of marriage is arranged though the society does not prefer it. In this type of marriage, till the ritual of *sindurdan* (putting of vermilion) in presence of the village *manjhi* (headman), *deheri* (priest), and relatives, marriage is not socially sanctioned. In such cases the wife is not eligible to attend/perform puja and even tabooed to take the consecrated food offered to the ancestors at *marha morpa*. During *sindurdan*, a feast is given to the relatives, guests and friends.

In case the girl returns with her parents, then the boy's party after 10 to 15 days, gives similar visit to the girl's house with sari, blouse, petticoat, and some ornaments including ring, garland etc. The boy's mother performs the similar rituals by massaging mustard oil, combing hair and giving the presentations to the girl with blessings. It is known as *pindha orha.* The bride price is fixed on that day. Bride price is known as *takaganda* or *neg niyam.* Traditionally bride price was only Rs. 2/= which was increased to Rs. 10/= to Rs. 15/=. Now a days it has increased to Rs. 200/= to Rs. 300/=, along with it the bridegroom's party has to bear the expenditure of grand feast given during marriage. There are several other expenditures. There is a story behind it.

A tiger once caught a man when he was drinking water from a stream in the forest. He requested the tiger to wait and to give him time to drink water. The tiger was kind enough and allowed him to drink water. After that the man again requested the tiger to leave him at the cost of his daughter whom he will send soon to the tiger. The tiger believed and set him free. Afterwards the man as per his promise sent his daughter to the tiger. When the tiger attacked the girl, her maternal uncle, uncle, brother, sister and the *deheri* arrived there. The sister threw a sari on the tiger and mislead it, the maternal uncle gave the tiger a goat, her brother attacked the tiger with a *tangi* (axe), the *deheri* kept the tiger far from the girl by chanting *mantra*s. In this way seven members rescued the girl from the tiger. So customarily during marriage, those relatives are given same items. The bridegroom's party has to give a *mai sari,* a *bahen sari*, a *bhai tangi*, and a *saladhara* or towel to the bride's brother, a turban to the uncle, a she goat to the maternal uncle, *gaon pasari* to the *deheri* at the time of entrance to the bride's village, some amount for bride's friends, expenditure of *pochai* needed in bride's house on the day of marriage, nine pieces of turmeric, nine *pai* of paddy grain, nine *pa*i of mustard oil, are also to be given to the bride's family.

Now a days the expenditure is curtailed and only Rs. 14/= is given to the Deheri who equally divide the amount among the claimants (rescued the girl from the tiger) as per the folklore.

Fixation of Marriage date – Generally marriage is performed within 15 days to one month after the finalization of marriage, which is sometimes delayed even upto 2 to 3 years. It depends on the economic condition of the bridegroom's family. The boy's side fixes the date, as they have to arrange expenditure for the marriage. The boy's parents, *deheri* and five other males of the village may be their relatives sit together in the courtyard. A plate is kept in front of them filled with water. They leave some paddy grains in the water and stir the water. When two grains touch with each other, they take the two and keep on a mango leaf. This process repeats for three times. Then they take a thread and colour it with *hawaid* (turmeric). The thread ties those three mango leaves separately one after another. They tie a number of gathans or shot. It is done to count the marriage date. If the marriage to be celebrated after 10 days, then there will be ten *gathans*. After each and every day one *gathan* will be untied. Then the Sirthu is sent to the girl's house with that. If the girl's family has any objection, they request for another suitable date.

Marriage rituals are performed at the bride's house preferably during morning. It is better to marry before the noon. A *maroa* is erected by four bamboo logs on which *sakhoa* leaves are spread. At the center another bamboo log is erected. Beside this a pitcher filled with water is kept. It is brought on the day of marriage early in the morning. Deheri accompanies the procession. Anointing mud mixed with cow dung paste purifies the place under the *maroa*.

The bridegroom's party starts for the bride's house very early in the morning. On the way the bridegroom has to marry a mango tree. He puts vermilion on it and ties a thread around it for three to five times. Similarly the bride is married with a mahua tree. This custom is known as *am biha* and *mahul biha*. It is believed that if there is any danger including death for the couple after marriage, it will happen to the tree with whom the first marriage is done and in this way they neutralize the crises if any.

Just before the entry in the village, at the entrance, the bridegroom's *deheri* is given a red chicken, which he sacrifices at the boundary and the blood is sprinkled there. This is known as Gaon Puja.Through this ritual he drives out all the evil spirits and purifies the village. He in this way binds the village and obstructs all the evil spirits to enter and interfere in that auspicious occasion. Then the bridegroom's party crosses the boundary and enters in the village. They bring two pitchers full with water with them, sprinkle water from it on the bridegroom's head and proceed to the bride's house. When they reach there the bride's party obstructs them and a mock fight between the two parties will happen and after paying some money, the bridegroom's party is allowed to enter the bride's house. At first the bridegroom's party sprinkles water on the bride's head. Then the bridegroom, who is brought by his elder sister's husband on his shoulder, stands near the pandal. The girl's mother and aunts also stand there holding a plate where a burning lamp, an arrow, a little quantity of mustard oil, some mango leaves, *dubba* and paddy grains are kept. They anoint mustard oil on a pair of leaves, heat those in the lamp and then massage that oil on the leaves on the bridegroom's face. Then they enter the *marua*. The bridegroom's father or uncle sits there keeping the bridegroom on his lap facing the east. Sitting on lap and riding on shoulder-these indicate that traditionally child marriage was the rule. Similarly the bride is brought and made to sit on her father or uncle's lap facing the west. The bride has to wear yellow sari. Yellow is a very auspicious colour to them. She also wears silver ornaments. Deheri officiates the marriage rituals. The ritual of *sindurdan*, which is the most important item among the rituals, is performed during the morning within 10 A.M. The *deheri* gets Rs.21/= as his remuneration which is known as *rash danga.* Then a feast is given to the relatives, guests and invitees. Presentations are given to the newly married couple. Next day early in the morning the bridegroom's party starts with the newly married couple to their village. Similar rituals of sacrifice of chicken and sprinkling of its blood on the village boundary are done for the protection of the village from all the evils. Then the couple enters the main room, salutes the ancestors placed in the *marha morpa* and all other deities established in and outside the room. Some persons of the family then cook food. The bride adds salt, turmeric in it. After the cooking is completed, the bride has to offer it to the ancestors at *marha morpa*. Then she serves it to all present there.

Ut Mangala - On the eighth day the couple visits the wife's parent's house. They take some vessel filled up with *pochai* for the wife's family. After drinking the liquor, a portion is poured on the ground where the marriage rituals are performed. Then staying there for one or two days they return to the in-law's village. Starting from the day of negotiation, till **Ut Mangala** - the ritual visit of newly married couple to the wife's house there are several rituals performed in both the houses.

Divorce - Divorce, referred as *chhara chhinda*, is allowed for both the sexes due to following grounds: when the wife is involved in adultery, lazy, quarrelsome, suspected as witch, etc. and when a husband is also questioned, is lazy, cruel, irresponsible, and unable to earn to maintain the family. In divorce, each of the couple simply tears a sal leaf and with that they are separated. The wife's party has to return the bride price and some other expenditure spent by the bridegroom's family during marriage.

Remarriage - Remarriage is allowed for both the sexes. A widow/ widower can marry again. In their cases, junior levirate or bhojai chumaona and junior sororate or sali chumaona are preferred most. When a widow marries her husband's younger brother, there is no question of return of bride price and some other expenditures but when she marries outside, her would be husband has to pay some amount as prescribed in their customary law and also as mutually decided by the community elders. The bride wears a new sari. The *sindurdan* ritual is done by any of the women present there instead of her husband. After marriage she simply follows her new husband and starts a new married life. Remarriage of a divorced and separated woman is allowed but in case the wife, her second husband has to pay some amount to the wife's father as bride price and other expenditures.

Pre marital and extra marital relationship - In all the cases the person and sometimes his / her family is excommunicated or becomes *jatgucha* and for re-entry the person or the family has to pay a *dand* (fine) to the society. If a Mal Paharia boy or a girl marries outside his or her own community, or has such relationship with a person outside the community, then the panch outcasts the person and the family. The family has to pay a *dand* (fine) for re-entry in the society. If a Mal Paharia marries in other community, then the family is excommunicated or becomes *jatgucha.* Then the parents have to pay the *dand*, which is generally 10 kgs. (20 *pai*) of rice grain, *dal* (pulses), a *bakra* (he goat), and 5 bottles of *mahua* liquor. With the celebration of a grand feast, the community accepts and includes the family among them but the boy or the girl- the offender is not accepted by the society. If a girl wants to come back and wants her reentry in the community, then her parents have to pay at least 30 kgs or 3 *soli* of rice, 10 bottles of liquor, dal or pulses and at least 3 goats. She has to promise in front of their *jati panch*, that she will never keep any connection with the person for whom she was excommunited. Otherwise the *panch* will not allow her to enter the community. Her parents are not allowed to keep any connection with her.

Case-1- Late Badrinath's daughter Soni was married with a Muslim boy. After a few days she returned to her parent's house and paying a fine; she was allowed to enter the community. Till date she has no connection with that Muslim fellow.

Case-2-During fieldwork, the researchers came to know that a meeting was going to be held in the village on an issue of an extra marital relationship. The meeting was held at about 12 noon after two days at a place under a mahua tree at the outskirt of the village. It was a case of a young Mal Paharia girl who became widow after a few years of her marriage. Her husband expired very recently. Then she returned to her natal village. After a few days, she got an extra marital relationship with a married person of the Ghatwar community. Some young Mal Paharia boys once them caught red handed during night in a vacant *jhupri* (hut). The girl's family was immediately excommunicated and a fine was imposed on them. A meeting was arranged between the two communities. Both the Mal Paharia and Ghatwar panchayats sat together along with the guilty and their parents. In that meeting, the village panchayat leader-the Pradhan who belonged to the Santal community was also invited and he joined. At the meeting, the boy and the girl were asked whether they want to live together or not. Both of them denied to continue that socially illegal relationship and were sorry for that. Then it is suggested that if they are again found to have such relationship with each other or with any other person, then Rs. 1000/= will be taken as a compensation by the *panch* from each of them and would be excommunicated for ever. At that time liquor was distributed among all present there, which was arranged by both the parties.

After three to four days again a meeting was held separately in each of their respective hamlets. It was the meeting in connection with *jat bhitar karna* and its expenditure was borne by the respective families. In the Pahariya tola the girl's parents had to pay 3 *soli* or 30 kgs. of rice, 15 bottles of liquor, and three he goats by which a grand feast was organized and the Mal Paharias of the village were fed. The village Pradhan belonging to the Santal community also attended the meeting and also had taken part in the grand feast.

It is observed that, some Mal Paharia have taken Christianity as their religion who are allowed to marry outside their own community and also can interdine with members of other communities also. In such cases, they first perform marriage in Church as per Christian rule. Then they return home and they perform all the rituals of marriage of the community including *sindurdan.*

Sindur (vermilion) is the marriage symbol. Widows are not allowed to put *sindur* and wear glass bangles. Instead of that they wear iron bangles.

Death

It is noted that the Mal Pahariyas always avoid talking on death. Death as usual like other communities of the world (with a little exception) is a very sorrowful event. The Mal Paharia is always very suspicious in any case of death happening in their village. As a reason for death, at first they suspect that this may be some evil act of mischievous spirits or caused by some malevolent act of some person.

Whenever a death occurs in a family of their society, the family members go to the village sorcerer cum medicineman or *ojha* (magician) or *Jan guru* (witch doctor). He takes a quantity of mustard oil on a sal leaf, which is rubbed on the leaf, and at the same time through his magical chanting he ascertain the exact reason of death. They have their own cremation and burial ground in the jungle. In case of unnatural death it is buried and others are cremated. In such cases many times quarrels break out in the society even sometimes it extends to murder. Generally they believe that there are *dains* who are responsible for the death of a child or young persons etc. Sometimes the *dain* is driven out of the village and severely tortured resulting even to killing. The cases of deaths occurred due to Small pox, Cholera, Diarrohea, death of a woman during her menstrual cycle, during pregnancy, childbirth, a breast-feeding child, a child prior to the performance of the *handipoda* ritual and death due to some accidents regarded as unnatural death. In such cases, the dead body is not cremated but buried. They have their own cremation and burial ground in the jungle. After the dead body is buried, the party who accompanied the dead proceeds to the deceased person's house. As they reach there, all of them are offered flour of maize known as *sattu* without salt to eat. The deceased person's family from that day observes pollution period for five days. During this period they abstain from taking salt, oil, spices and non-vegetarian food. On the fifth day, the barber comes to pare nails of the family members and all their cognate male members shave the beard and head. The other Mal Paharia of the village also pare their nails and take shaving of their beard and head. Then all of them take purificatory bath. After that they take sattu of maize, *murhi* or puffed rice, *chura* or flattened rice added with salt. On the next day the family members feed all the relatives and friends. This time the invitees are fed with *sattu*, *murhi* and *chura and dal or* pulses without salt. Non-vegetarian food and liquor are not given in this ritual feast. The soul of such a deceased person is not brought to the *marha morpa* (the place regarded as resting place of the deceased souls).

Those, whose death is regarded as natural death, are again divided into two categories. The deceased persons, whose family is unable to arrange ritual feast to the invitees, are cremated keeping the head at the southern direction. In such cases, they only arrange to feed the persons who accompanied the funeral party. They will only be given a ritual feast, on the sixth day, consisting only *sattu* added with salt. In this way they overcome the pollution period.

If any death occurs inside the room, the room gets polluted and they have to dismentle the room and it will be newly constructed. After a person dies, all the villagers, relatives, and friends assemble there in that house. Women members of the lineage massage the dead body with oil and salt. Then dead body is wrapped with a new white cloth. Then four persons from the gathering are selected who are considered as not polluted. Here purity signifies for a person who is having no type of pollution such as birth, death, wife of such a man neither is pregnant nor passing through her menstrual cycle. Those four persons are selected to carry to act as pallbearer and they carry the dead in a bier up to the funeral ground. They keep a piece of tile or *khapra* or some *kher* grass from the thatch by which the room is thatched on the bier. A person walks in front of the pallbearers by sprinkling cereals and grains such bajra, makai, and dhan in the way up to the cremation ground. In the cremation ground they arrange the pyre with wood. The dead body is laid on it placing the head in the north direction (except those who are not able to arrange the cost of ceremonial feast as described earlier). Then generally the eldest son singes the mouth of the dead at cremation. Then all other persons one by one put fire on the pyre. The bier is then broken by any of the four persons who carried the dead. The person who torches the dead body's mouth is not allowed to see the face of the deceased person during his performacce. He puts fire on the dead from his back in the way of keeping his hands at the back. The funeral party after cremation comes to the nearby water source and they all take bath and proceed to the deceased person's village. On their way to the hamlet just at the entrance a person stands with mustard oil, *kancha halud* (turmeric), and *sattu* of *makai.* They all massage oil on the body, face, hands and feet. The makai is burnt and the rest of the things are baked and those are touched on their body. Thereafter they reach to the deceased person's house. Each of them is offered a plate with *makai sattu* and a *dona (*leaf cup) with water. They all go to the place where the deceased is cremated and offer those in the name of the deceased person and return to the deceased person's house. There they are offered dried turmeric paste mixed with mustard oil and touched by hansia (an iron agricultural implement). They anoint the paste on their hands, feet, face and whole body. Each of them is offered a lota (small vessel) of water to wash their hands and mouth. Now the person who torched the deceased person's mouth, prepares *sattu* without salt. They do not take turmeric and salt on that day. Next day the party again goes to the cremation ground to locate if any unburnt piece is there. If there is any such piece found they immediately burn that and then return to the deceased person's house and prepare *makai sattu* added with salt (slightly excess) and distribute it to each and every Pahariya family of the village. The deceased person's family abstains from taking non-vegetarian food for eight days. On the eighth day they assemble to the place where the person died. There they cook rice and pulses. They burn a chicken in fire and then it is cooked in a new pot. They keep those distributing in seven leaf plates and offer those to the deceased person in the cremation ground. They put some coin in each of the plates. The barber takes the coins. Then all of them take purificatory bath and with that, except the deceased person's family and close consanguine, all other persons are freed from pollution.

The pollution period for the family and close kins lasts for twelve days. Earlier it was one month. It sometimes even extends to one year depending upon the strength to accumulate money for expenditure of the feast. For twelve days they abstain from taking any type of non-vegetarian food including *masur dal,* onion, garlic etc. They also are tabooed to take food added with *chhoka* (spices singed in oil or ghee which is to be mixed with any cooked dish by reboiling). On the twelvth day they call the barber to pare their nails, shave head and beard of the entire close consanguines and then they all take the purificatory bath. After that they prepare a chicken and a he goat and mix with *makai sattu.* Those are distributed among the persons present there.

On the twelfth day they cut a chicken and a he-goat outside the house. This is known as *bail para.* Then they return to the deceased person's house. The head of the he-goat is cooked with rice and offered in three leaf plates in the name of the deceased person. The *lapit* or barber takes one leg of the he-goat. Rest of the meat is then divided into three shares. The villagers who accompanied the funeral procession take one share, the owner of the sacrificed animal takes one share and rest is equally shared and taken by four pallbearers.

Another goat is then slaughterd, which is known as *onsh* or *onyech* (chhut or pollution) *guchad* (nikalna or overcome). The meat is cooked by the villagers and distributed among all present there. The whole ritual is known as *pata sija* through which they all become pollution free and are also allowed to take non-vegetarian food. Though the family is allowed to take non-vegetarian food but is not allowed to arrange marriage of any of the unmarried person of the family and their married women are tabooed to put *sindur*(vermilion) till the performance of *bhoj* or ceremonial feast.

They establish deceased person's soul in their *marha morpa* when it is a natural death. Each of the family members takes some salt, which is known as *nun khoa* they call the soul to come and stay with them and to take rest in the *marha morpa* instead of roaming helter-skelter. On this occasion they take a chicken, offer it a quantity of rice grain and allow it to take that. After the chicken takes atleast a few grains, they sacrifice it at the *marha morpa* in the name of the deceased soul, cook and offer it to the particular deceased person's soul along with others whose souls are already established. In this way they establish the deceased ancestor's soul in that particular place.

Mal Paharia followers of Sat Sangh do not maintain *marha morpa*. They believe this is nothing but only superstition like others such as practising of witchcraft, belief in ghosts and other spirits. All these are the evils for their society, which bring unhappy situation in their society. They observe pollution period as per their social norms. As they are strictly vegetarians they do not perform any animal sacrifice while other rituals are performed. They abstain from consuming oil, spices and salt as per the Mal Paharia norms, do not perform any ritual during the pollution period and get rid of all types of pollutions by celebrating a *bhoj* (a ceremonial feast).

The Christian Mal Paharia buries their dead as per the Christian norms. And on returning home they also follow their social norms. Both the norms (Christian and Mal Paharia) are accommodated in their practices. It varies from person-to-person, family-to-family but no Christian family is found who install or preserve *marha morpa* in their house.

7

Survival Strategy: Use of Traditional Knowledge in Health Care Practices

The majority of population that lives in forests are tribal communities. They have developed a way of life, which is woven and cherished around forest ecology and forest resources. Forests have been their well loved home for centuries. It is the abode of their mother deity and it represents their whole way of life. The tribal communities could subsist for thousands of years from where they eke out their need for survival like food, water, drinks, shelter, clothes, medicines and occupational opportunity for employment etc. Thus the local tribal communities have a symbiotic relationship with forests and have a deep socio-cultural attachment with the forests. Each tribal group of our country has its own unique cultural heritage, which differs from that of the other.

With the passage of time, tribal untrammeled peaceful habitat has been disturbed with the increased commercial use of forest resources and exploitation of forests has increased manifold without corresponding to the regeneration and creation of man-made forests.

The great wealth of medicinal plants in the forests of our country has made her the pride home of Ayurvedic medicines since the Vedic age. Plants were thought to be the best weapons for combating ailments and as a preventive cure against diseases. Indigenous or folk form of such medicine is still in use in various corners of our country till date and especially in rural and tribal areas (Tiwari and others, 1998).

The traditional knowledge in regard to health care practices, which the tribal have acquired over generation, is the key source of inspiration of maintaining their livelihood in such forest environment (Dasgupta and Sarkar, 2005). Due to close association with forest the tribals are well aware of facing ailment through various local herbs, plants, roots and tubers and their various uses and parts of uses. The knowledge to use various local herbs and plants, fruits, roots and barks as medicinal value is very much restricted among a few members of the community which they have acquired from their ancestors and at present they are the living custodian of great intangible cultural heritage. Thus, this knowledge is very much local and it is very unique for a particular community for their sustainable living in such forest environment. This knowledge bank of rural India is gradually dwindling and shrinking due to rapid penetration of the various tenants of globalization.

From our empirical study it is revealed that Mal Paharia also possesses a good knowledge of their vegetation wealth of their vicinity and also use of various herbs and plants for their daily diet chart, which possess a good calorie and vitamin value. They are highly aware of their forest wealth, which they use, in their traditional rituals and ceremonies and in ailment in a sustainable manner and on the basis of their great traditional wisdom they also conserve the bio-diversity of their niche. Interestingly, their economy, cultural behaviour, religious beliefs and practices, norms and morals are all the product of traditional and intimate knowledge about the nature, natural product and natural phenomena (Dasgupta and Sarkar, 2005).

The knowledge among Mal Paharia to get rid of ailment through local herbs, plants, tubers, roots and barks etc. clearly suggests their belief and practices relating to health care and diseases, which are products of completely indigenous cultural developments. The present treatise is confined upon the Mal Paharia of Dumka district, Jharkhand, who exploit their immediate natural resources for their ailment. It is also observed that before application of medicine the *ojha* or *janguru* (sorcerer cum medicine man) try to understand the problem of patient through pulse beat by touching the pulse of the patient and which is followed by some magico- religious performances since Mal Paharia have a strong belief and cultural sentiment about various malevolent spirit of their vicinity usually believed to be responsible for various health problems. However, regarding application of herbal medicine they only depend on their *biro piyao* (baid) who is aged about 99 years at Madhuvan village.

Application of Traditional Knowledge for Ailment

Name of the Disease (Local Name/English Name)	***Use of Local Herbs***	***Application***
1. Penjon or Anatarba (Irregularity / or delay or pain in Menstruation	(a) Kalihari jaghdai (*Gloriosa superba)* or, (b) Kala datura/umman (*Datura fastuosa)* (c) Malkangni, kajuri/ chiron (*Celastrus paniculata)*	It's tuber is grounded and apply in the forehead for at least seven days. Flower of it is grounded and mix with molasses or honey and taken twice in a day It's tender leafs cut

		into pieces and are fried in mustard oil. One teaspoon of such is taken twice in a day for 15-20 days.
2. Shet Pradar (White ischarge)	(a) Baer fruit/ilantha (*Zizyphus jujuba*)	It's fruit is grounded and mix with molasses and taken twice in a day
	(b) Bark of neem tree (*Azadirachta indica)*	Bark is grounded into paste and mix with honey and taken one tea spoon twice in a day for a period of 10-12 days
	(c) Seed bark of imli (Tamarindus indica)	The outer coat of *imli* seed is grounded and mixes with sugar candy and taken ¼ tea spoon twice daily for 7 days.
3.Sthan-Rog (Lactation Problem)	(a) Tuber of satawar (*Asparagus raccmosus)*	Tuber of satawar is gounded and mixes with cow milk and then it is boiled for some time and taken twice in a day
	(b) Root of erand (*Ricinus communis*) and tuber of satawar (*Asparagus racemosus*)	Both the items with equal proportion is grounded and prepares a small pea size two tablet and mixes with sugar candy and

		taken twice in a day
4. Khasi (Cough)	Leaf of ishwarmul (*Aristolochia indica)*	Its leaf are grounded with honey and taken.
5. Rangbandh (High temperature with red rashes in the body)	(i) Root if bindhi/ lal bherenda (*Jatropha gossypifolia)*	Root of bindhi is grounded and apply in the affected region of the body.
	(ii) Root of anantamul/ dudhilata (*Ichnocarpus frutescens*), root of bhui champa (*Kaempferia rotunda*), root of gharundi sag (Alternanthera sessilis) and root if kantha bhaji/ acch adro (*Amaranthus spinosus)*	All are mixed with ghee of cow and boiled for a long time. Paste is applied as well as taken for 3 to 4 times in a day
	(iii) Flower of goalichi / gulanch (*Plumeria acutifolia*), root of chirchiti / chirchira (*Achyranthes aspera*) and leaf of gritakumari (*Aloe vera*)	All the three are mixed and grounded and paste is applied and also taken.
6. Ghav in new born's crown of the head (wound in newborn's crown of the head which is delightfully soft)	Dried Bones of tortoise and dried bark of *barka nimbu* (Pomelo)	Both are mixed and grounded into paste and apply on the surface of head of new born.
7. Udri (Dropsy)	Root of erandi/ castor oil plant (*Ricinus communis*), *bansim* (wild variety of bean) and lime of the oyster	These are mixed and grounded and consumed.
8. Nak sinjra (Cold)	Juice of velva/ bhilawa seed (*Semecarpus anacardium)*	Apply inside the nose the extracted juice of *velva* seed (unmatured)

9. Pilhoi (Malaria)	Root of *tijubala*, tuber of *tiput*, root of *ishwar muli* (*Aristolochia indica)*	These are mix with *gondh* and grounded and prepare tablet; and taken twice a day.
10. Lahu ghav (wound)	Root of chibal and palash (*Butea frondosa*)	(a) Root of both are grounded and paste is applied. (b) When the said paste is heated and applies on the wound, immediately the bleeding is stopped.
11. Pet dukhai (stomach-ache)	Root of champa(*Michelia champaca)*, ban kursa and rakti.	Root of the three plants are grounded with *Ishwar muli gadh* and prepare tablets (*goli*) which are dried in Sun ray and taken two *goli* at a time for a period of one month.
12. Sarpa bish (Snake bite) or Bichhu katna (Scorpion bite)	(a) Root of nagbael/ sarpa gandha (*Rauwolfia serpentina*) or Ishwar mul (*Aristolochia indica*)	Root of this plant is grounded and consumed and paste of such is apply on the wound.
	(b) Bark of palash (*Butea frondosa)*	Bark of palash and pieces of ginger are grounded and consumed.
	(c) Bark of charai gorba simkata/ nagpheni (*Vitex peduncularis*)	Bark of this plant is grounded into paste and consume as well as apply on the body

	(d) Seed of kursi (*Mucuna nivea*)	About 6-8 pieces of seed is grounded with water and taken.

Moreover, in order to protect their (Mal Paharia) houses from snakes, which are situated either in hill slopes or in the forest, they usually planted *airi* (*Pedilanthes tithymaloides*) and k*ebamba sangha/ kewa kanda* (*Costus speciosus*) in their *vitto* land.

13. Bichhu kata (Scorpion bite)	(a) Latex of Papita (Papaya) (*Carica papaya*)	Latex of *papita* is applied on the wound.
	(b) Juice of aonla (Phyllanthus emblica)	Juice of aonla is applied on the wound.
	(c) Leaf of sakarkanda (*Ipomoca batatas)*	Juice of leaf is applied and consumed.
	(d) Seed of karanj (*Pongamia glabra)*	Seed is crushed into paste and consumed
	(e) Tuber of kali musli (*Curculigo orchioides)*	Tuber is grounded with slight water and applies on the wound as well as consumed.
14. Paychese (Dysentry)	(a) Young leaf of phutkal (*Ficus infectoria)*	Young leaf of *phutkal* is boiled and it's water is consumed and also boiled leaf are taken three to four times in a day
	(b) Bark of sal tree (*Shorea robusta)*	Bark of *sal* is grounded and

		about one teaspoon of such powder is making paste on the hearth/oven and taken three times in a day. It also acts during blood dysentery.
	(c) Leaf and fruit of kukurbicha or seta bili / kucho bati (*Grewia hirsuta*)	Both leaf and fruit are crushed and boiled and a thick substance prepared, which is consumed three-four times in a day.
15. Kukur Khasi (Whooping cough)	(a) Leaf of ishwarmul (*Aristolochia indica*)	At the initial stage its young leaf as well as dried leaf are grounded with honey and taken four times in a day.
16. Kashra (Missals)	Thorns of semal (*Bombax ceiba*)	Thorn of *semal* is grounded with water and consumed.
17. Bukhar (Fever)	(a) Fruit and root of barhanta/ Indian night shade (*Solanum indicum)*	Both root and fruit of *barhanta* are grounded and boiled with water, and a thick substance is prepared (*karha*) and taken about two tea spoon at a time for two times in a day for five to seven days.

	(b) Leaf of harsinghar/ night jasmine (*Nyctanthes arbor-tristis)*	Young leafs are boiled into *karha* and taken about two tea spoon at a time for twice in a day
18. Haiza (Cholera)	Bark of jamun (*Enginia jambolana*), liquor of mahua* (*Bassia latifolia*) (*Phulli liquor is required which is of high alcohol concentration; during distillation of mahua flower for liquor, the first 20 minutes distillation is known as *phulli*).	Both are mixed and grounded and taken one teaspoon at every hour till recovery.
19. Sar dard (Headache)	(a) Bark of chilbil / churla (*Holoptelic integrifolia)* (b) Dried up twigs of akhwan/ akanda/barangobali (*Calotropis gigantea*).	The fresh bark of *chilbil/ churla* is tied on the forehead. Dried twigs are fired in inhaled like bidi smoking through nostrils.
20. Moch (Sprain)	(a) Latex of akhwan/ barangobali (*Calotropis gigantea)* (b) Bark of pojo/baglal (*Litsaea polyantha*) and oil of kujuri *(Celastrus paniculata*).	Latex of *akhwan* is mixed with salt and applies. Both are mixed and grounded into paste and applies.
21. Dama (Asthma)	(a) Leaf of ishwar mul (*Aristolochia indica)*	Firstly, young tender leafs are half dried in the sun ray and taken after food by chewing one leaf like betel leaf for a period of 12-15 days.

	(b) Root of lajwanti/ chui mui (*Mimosa pudica*) and fruit of loto/mainphal (*Randia dumetorum*)	Both are mixed and crushed into powder and mix with honey and taken about one teaspoon twice in a day.
22. High blood Pressure	(a) Fresh kunduri fruit (*Cephalandra indica*) and garlic	Fresh *kunduri* fruit is cut from middle put there a piece of garlic and chew the same in empty stomach at early morning.
	(b) Yellow leaves of sahijan or drumstick (*Moringa oleifera*)	Yellow leaves of drumstick are cooked with molasses and taken in empty stomach at early morning.
23. Low blood pressure	(a) Leaves of charaigorba	Young leaves are boiled and consumed as like tea.
	(b) Noni Sak (*Portulaca quadrifida*)	Leaves of it are prepared like a soup and taken twice in a day.

24. Masuro ka dard (Gum problem)	(i) Bark of kumbhi (*Carea arborea*) or Bark of amarbel (*Cuscuta reflexa)* (ii) Root of bhui champa (*Kaempferia rotunda*), kamraj (*Butteneria herbacea*) and bhengraj (*Eclipta alba*).	Bark is mixed with water and prepares a *karha* by boiling and the pour into mouth for rinse. All the three roots are mixed and ground and then as a paste applies.
25. Danth dard (Toothache)	(a) Root and Bark of koreya (*Holarrhena antidysenterica)* (b) Root of ishwarmul (*Aristolochia indica*)	After grinding of both with water it is applied to the affected tooth. Fresh root is washed and chew in the mouth and juice with saliva is applied on the affected tooth.
26. Khujli (Eczyma)	Chirata/ kalmegh/mahamage plant (*Andrographis paniculata*).	The whole plant is soaked in water and water is consumed.
27. Khujli, boil and pimple with pain	Fruit of *pitrin* tree	The fruit is rubbed in a stone slab and the paste applies.
28. Piliya (Jaundice)	Seed of the fruit of *pitrin* tree	In case of *piliya* (or jaundice) the seeds of the fruit is used as series for wearing as necklace.
29. Ban bish gethia bath (Joints gout)	Leaves having twelve nodes, fruit of *ralli*, root of *ralli*, bark of *patnopa*, bark of *ashariya*, bark of *rohin*, *goalki* (black pepper-procure from local market), *anantamul*, bark of *chatni* and *jaiphal* (procure from market)	All these are cut into pieces and pounded and consume one teaspoon twice in a day.

30. Raat kana (Night blindness)	Ghogol (dove bird) available in the agricultural field	The sap collects from the anal region of *ghogol* and applies 6 to 8 drops in the eye for 3 to 4 times in a day.
31.Jhala pardho/ badhak (Irregular menstruation)	Bark of *rohini,* bark of *patnopa, semul* flower, *akhwan/akanda* flower, *mach kuda* fruit, *jaba phool (*china rose) , root of *raipan, ashariya* and *kedar rahet*, seed of *kanoyek jang* (it is a creeper),*himsagar* (looks like a yellow leaf), root of *kend mahakkal,bansim, ban kapas* and *majur jhuti* root, flower of *parat.*	All these are mix and cut into pieces and pounded and then grinded to form tablet and consumed daily 2 to 3 times; non-vegetarian food is not allowed during this period and leafy vegetable- *purai* is also tabooed during this period.
32. Sardi-khasi (Cold and cough)	Leaves of sajina (*Moringa oleifera)*, garlic (*Allium sativum)* and salt.	Leaves of *sajina* are boiled for prolong time and then its water is mix with salt and garlic and again boiled; after that the hot drink is consumed and get relief.

Mal Paharia as well as other local inhabitants in their vicinity depend on traditional medicinal plants for several reasons; of which the main ones are poverty, lack of availability of medical services in their rural area, which are secluded with poor communication. They are compelled to use traditional therapy through local medicinal practitioner or baid (*biropiyao*). The basic thrust of our study in this arena is furthering understanding, awareness and importance of existing traditional healthcare practices among the Mal Paharia.

Thus, it is revealed from above discussion that Mal Paharia living in this ecological set-up relied upon traditional knowledge for centuries; on the basis of such local knowledge handed down from ascending generation where it is built upon, modified and refined to suit present circumstances. But today, this vast knowledge bank is eroding fast and much has been already lost with tenants of modernization and globalization where the rapid spread of foreign technology with money introduced from outside.

9

Observation and Conclusion

It appears from the foregoing discussion on the Mal Paharia of Dumka district of Jharkhand that their life and culture are still nourished in the lap of nature and as a result the nature of material objects and material way of living, possessed by the Mal Paharia often considerably directed by their immediate natural environment.

Mal Paharias are settled within the boundary of Damin-i-Koh. From the studied sample it is evident that the rate of illiteracy is very much higher i.e. about 54%. Though among the younger generation (i.e. 11-40 yrs) the rate of literacy is 26.86% between both the sexes, which clearly suggest that younger generations are inclined towards the value of education. The average family size is considerably medium i.e. 5.91 persons which indicates that due to uncertainty in their life, the size of the family is affected. More so, it is also observed that in 22 households out of 56 households of the studied Madhuvan village of Gopikandar block there were patients of Kala-azar and Malaria, which affects the population size of the respective Mal Paharia families. For Kala-azar a kind of fly is responsible. During our field investigation in 2006-07 it is found that a drain was under construction at this village on this hilly terrain which is simply wastage of government fund because the villagers use the drain for their deification which not only pollutes the environment but it becomes a very suitable breeding place of the flies which is also one of the reason for spreading Kala azar in this area. A jeepable road is under construction from the foothills village- Ormo and the expenditure is met out from the grant of World Bank; in this road construction work Mal Paharia people of the village are involved.

The Mal Paharia is primarily *kurao* (slash and burn) cultivators but with the advent of time and their interaction with immediate neighbour the Santal, they have also adopted the technique of settled cultivation. According to their emic perception they have categorized their cultivable land for varieties of crops and cereals, which are already mentioned. The role of moneylenders in their area was very much active but now a days it is interfared by AAA (Agrarian Assistance Association) – a NGO of Dumka. AAA is actively involved in developing their economy by household food security (i.e. the practice of proper management of natural resources, sustainable practice of agriculture by use of organic manure in indigenous technique; selection of traditional seeds instead of using hybrid varieties, and as well as practice of multi crop. At the same time knowledge is being imparted for preservation as well as promotion of their bio-diversity through forest protection, wasteland development. The most remarkable observation has been made during our field investigation at Madhuvan that at the village grass root level AAA people are devoted to empower women folk among the Mal Paharia through Mahila Gram Sabha. In this regard a detail description has already been made. Most of the women among the Mal Paharia are involved in project tranning organised by AAA, as well as they also earn for their family and often during crisis they take loan from Mahila Gram Sabha instead of local moneylender whose rate of interest is too high.

It has been observed that schooling of children is not regular rather their attendance in the school is only for mid-day meal, and in preparing they are busy in most of time of their school. Therefore, it is suggested that residential schooling with ensured regular supply of ration to all and regular payment of salary to the teacher in those school should be ensured by local administration.

The **Birsa Abas Yojna** should be extended to all Mal Paharia families considering their customary law for house making, i.e. keeping a provision of sacred place – **Marha Morpa**. It is observed that fund released from Government of India for developmental activities for the Primitive tribal Groups is successfully implemented in the name of Birsa Abas yojna among the Mal Paharia of Upar Murgathali village while it is abscent in our other studied villages. It is reported during our empirical study in January, 2007 that there are 39 Mal Paharia beneficiaries at Upar Murgathali village who has received Rs.56000/= for construction of house under Birsa Abas Yojana scheme. The houses have cemented brick wall, false ceiling with angle, where the roof is of *poyal*(straw) and tile, iron door and window. While there are another group of beneficiaries (three in number) who has received Rs.25000/= for house construction in the same schme which are of *kachha* type, mud wall, made of bamboo with tiles.

It is also observed that in the catchment area of Upar Murgathali village there should be reservour, which will serve the purpose of irrigation during lean agricultural season especially for Rabi crop.

The role of other NGO like **PRADAN (Professional Assistance for Development Action)** is also found significant towards development of the subsistence level by earning money through the seeds of cocoon (silk worm) in which a group of persons are involved forming a chain and before supplying such cocoon seeds those are thoroughly examined under a microscope and a person among them is already trained in this aspect from **PRADAN**.

The penetration of modern market economy in their daily life is evident from the use of various brands of soaps and detergent, as well as importance of money get accelerated among them which is marked from their attendance at weekly market. With the help of media like Television, Radio and folk media like public announcement in the market the child immunization as well as vaccination programme is accepted but due to their secluded habitat in the hilly terrain they are often unable to avail of such facilities in time. It is also observed in the Madhuvan village that **GTFI** (Golden Trust Financial Insurance Company) has penetrated in this hilly terrain among the Mal Paharia; some of their Mal Paharia agents are Aditya, Sonai, Kapil, Rajiv and Rajendra who live in Madhuvan village. But the Mal Paharia are very much ignorant of various pros and cons of such insurance and if some among them are trapped without knowing the details of investment, then it would be another curse to them like taking loan from local money lender. Therefore, local administration should initiate their intervention in order to avoid harassment to Mal Paharia in future. With the help of NGO's Self Help Group (SHG) especially among women are being encouraged and in various Mal Paharia villages it is very much active.

Since they are living in the lap of nature they are highly aware of use of herbs, plants and roots during any kinds of ailment; but when it is failed they usually consult *janguru* (witch doctor) among the Santal. When they fail to cure, only then they approach for local government hospital.

II

With the rise of population among the Mal Paharia the land-man ratio is lessened among them, which indirectly affects their subsistence activity. The educated young generation among them are highly aware of their glorious past when their area of economic operation was on the land in the plain area which is now-a-days no longer in their possession and in majority of the cases occupied by the Santals and due to such their grievances are noticed towards their immediate neighbour – the Santals – who are *diku* (outsider) to them and are the beneficiaries of all government scheme depriving them.

Authors also came across from the studied villages of the Mal Paharia that Paharia were not only hostile but warrior group during British period. The then British force was compelled to leave the place called *danga para* due to the pressure under the leadership of Jama Paharia. He was from Kumarbhag Paharia, and was also known as Jabra Majhi or Tilka Majhi during Paharia revolt in 1750. During our empirical study we have interviewed a number of old Paharia people as well as elite members at Dumka and came to know that a section of Santal claim Tilka Majhi as their own community member. In the context of Santals, Mal Paharia informants are of opinion that the Santals of this area pushed Paharia people to forested hilly terrain where lands are undulated and non-irrigated; in fact Santals are enjoying the best quality of land in the plain area of *damin-i-koh* till date. The young generation of Mal Paharia are not only annoyed or expressed their continuous angry grumble in this issue and also consider Santal of their territory as *diku* (outsider) and they say that the Santals are trying to grab their glorious heritage by propagating Tilka Majhi as their community member. There is a possibility of disharmony in near future in this territory, which may aggravate in the light of globalisation.

Due to prolong association with their Hindu neighbour, especially Bengali, their language has been changed remarkably especially the vocabulary.

It is also revealed that the Mal Paharia are found to establish a close relationship with the spiritual world either by controlling or overpowering the spirit by enchanting or practising some rituals. They try to control the power for good or bad by offering sacrifice, rituals etc. to propitiate the supernatural power for acquisition of desired object. Their life and culture are very much governed by various malevolent and benevolent spirits and the symbolic expressions of these collective sentiments, which are regulated, maintained and are transmitted over generations, control the total mode of social cohesion among them. They also worship various Hindu deities like, Brahma, Vishnu, Parvati, Lakshmi, Ganga, Tulsi, and Hanumanji etc. along with their own deities. A few among them are the followers of a reformist group of religion, i.e. Satsangh and a very few are converted as Christian; again it is due to their orthodox social system in which there is a concept of *dayen* (witch) is prevalent. Along with the religious beliefs and practices of the Christianity the studied Christian Mal Paharias still cannot totally leave all of their age-old practices.

The Mal Paharia after a prolong interaction with their Hindu neighbours have adopted many of Hindu rites-rituals. They practise those along with their age-old belief system. It is also ascertained that they may be a stock from Dravidian origin, migrated to this part of country due to maladjustment with their brethren advanced Dravidian fellow. This group was in favour of forest dwelling culture and migrated to this part of Rajmahal hills in remote past and was nature worshipper, which still continues (Biswas, 2005). However, in course of time they have adapted many local rites and rituals at this place of *damin-i-koh*.

III

Consequently with the advent of new world economy which is supported by advanced technology, competitions, flow of capital etc. along with fast changing social values, the socio-cultural life, the traditional knowledge system of Mal Paharia-a secluded tribal group will definitely be affected. As a result the tribal group especially tribal people of the hilly terrain will be in soup in the new emerging competitive social-cultural environment, which is the outcome of tenents of globalisation.

The globalisation process has also affected Mal Paharia society and culture and as a result the socio-cultural change among the Mal Paharia can be conceived through dialectical-historical approach of Marx. Infact "Marx noted five stages of social differentiation, viz"

(i) tribal community with undivided property in land and agriculture in common,

(ii) disintegration of tribal community and its transformation into family communities with loosening of common property,

(iii) land shares being fixed by inheritance rights or the degree of kinship, thus creating inequality; tribals are further increase this inequality.

(iv) passing of inequality based kinship to that on possession as expressed by actual cultivation,

(v) system of periodical redistribution of communal land, and its gradual shrinking, first this redistribution included house land, arable land and pasture but gradually the sphere of communal property shrank and was limited only to the community woodland and waste. Such progressive differemntiation of property in ancient and medieval India also logically inheres for Marx the unfolding of the rest of the historical forces of change and its march to subsequent stages of social transformation" (Singh, 1989).

Apart from this, the dialectical-historical concepts for the study of social change through the idea of Ramakrishna Mukherjee (1965) can also be considered in the present context.

Accordingly the above study on the Mal Paharia group of people of the studied villages shows that in spite of having their rigid age-old traditions they are not lagging behind. On the contrary due to culture contact with people of other societies, religions, with advance technology and educations, they, especially the elite group among them eagerly have taken the views, techniques etc. from others for their economic development, to stop their beliefs and practices in relation to the evils in their religious practices. At the same time it is observed that due to contacts with their Hindu neighbours they have adapted many of their deities and their rituals sometimes in their own way and sometimes together with them. In fact they are standing on the bridge where one end is full of their traditional belief system while, the other end is adaption of some Hindu deities in order to show their neighbour a kind of respect and obedience, which often may be the result of the fusion of these two.

IV

It appears that concept of globalisation is the result of global connectivity through which social changes are being produced by the dynamics of capitalist development as well as diffusion (Mondal, 2006). Here in the Mal Paharia field situation globalisation also encourages cultural and social identities. The new means of communication also empowers Mal Paharia at this vicinity for enhancing cultural interaction with the outsiders. Thus the global cultural changes also affected their age-old traditions and changes have come in certain spheres. But it does not imply the total change of traditional system by a new one. The Mal Paharias still possess strong belief system and changes that are observed among them are found only in the periphery of their culture that is especially on the material aspect of the culture. Therefore, the tenents of globalisation among the Mal Paharia is the extension of modernisation, which includes transformation in the sphere of economic, social and cultural level leaving aside their deep-rooted religious belief system. However, the Mal Paharia is very much inclined towards materialistic life, which is manifested in consumerism and individualism. Therefore, global influence on this local culture has penetrated in their behaviour pattern. Due to such their rich knowledge bank for ailment being a tool for survival strategy in such environments are liable to malfunction. Their coping mechanism are no longer adequate to meet the changed socio-cultural environment while this great knowledge repository is again having a potential industrial and commercial application. Necessary awareness is required to protect indigenous intellectual property rights(IPR). Lastly, we have observed there is a symbiotic relation between forests and the Mal Paharia tribe but due to advent of globalisation process in this area the protection of entire eco-system is not at all ensured as cutting and destructioin of forests is a regular feature. The inhabitants of this area took forests as a renewable resource and they live by cutting down the forest for subsistence and income. Ultimately, the forest dwelling tribe like Mal Paharia become the victims of developmental programme, which benefit only a section of people of the area.

Bibliography

Appadurai, Arjun, 2000, "Grassroots Globalization and the Research Imagination", in *Public Culture*, Vol.12, No. 1, pp. 12-19.

Bailey, F.G., 1960, *Tribe, Caste and Nation*, Delhi : Oxford University Press.

Biswas, Sushanta, 2005, *Mal Paharia* (in Bengali), Calcutta : Loko Sanskriti O Adibasi Sanskriti Kendra, Govt. of West Bengal.

Bose, N.K., 1961, *Cultural Anthropology*, Bombay : Asia Publishing House.

Dalton, E.T., 1872, *Descriptive Ethnology of Bengal*, Calcutta : Office of the Superintendent of Government of India.

Das, A.K., B. Roychowdhury & M.K. Raha 1966 *The MalPaharia of WestBengal*, Calcutta : Bulletin of the Cultural Rcscarch Institute, Tribal Welfare Dept., Govt. of West Bengal (Sp. Series No.7).

Das, N.K., 2006, "Perspective of Religious Syncretism: A Critique of Conceptions of Culture" : in *Humankind*, Vo.2, pp.87-123.

Elwin, V., 1941, *The Loss of Nerves*, Oxford Pamphlets of Indian Affairs, No.14, Oxford: Oxford University Press.

Griffiths, W.G., 1946, *The Kol Tribes of Central India*; Calcutta : The Royal Asiatic Society of Bengal.

Lal, R.B., 1988, *District Census Handbook, Census of India, 1981*, Series – 4, Bihar, Part – XIII-A, Village and Town Directory, Bihar : Director of Census Operation.

Mondal, Sekh Rahim, 2006, "Cultural Globalization and Globalization of Culture – Some Observations" in *The Oriental Anthropologist.* Vol.6, No.2, pp. 297-306.

Mookherjee, Bhabandana, 1981, *Structure and Kinship in Tribal India,* Calcutta: Minerva Associates (Publications) Pvt. Ltd.

Mukherjee, Ramakrishna, 1965, The Sociologist and Social Change in India Today, Delhi, Prentice Hall of India.

O'malley, L.S.S., 1910, *Bengal District Gazetteers* : Santal Parganas, Calcutta : The Bengal Secretariat Book Depot.

Prasad, Binod Mohan and S.P. Singh, 1989, *Santal Parganas Tenancy Mannual*, Patna : Malhotra Bros.

Risley, H.H., 1891, *The Tribes and Castes of Bengal*, Calcutta: Bengal Secretariat Press.

Raovallurupalli, Sivaji, 2009, The Global India, Delhi: Agam Kala Prakashan

Sahay, K.N., 1967, 'A Study in the Process of Transformation from Tribe to Caste, Parhaiyas of Lolki-a case Study, in *Journal of Social Research,* Vol.X, No.1, Ranchi.

Sahay, K.N., 1976 Under the Shadow of the cross: A Study of the Network and Processes of Christianization among the Uraon of Central India, Calcutta: Institute of Social Research and Applied Anthropology.

Sinha, S.C., 1962, "State Formation and Rajput Myth in Tribal Central India", *Man in India*, Vol. 42, pp. 35- 80.

Singh, Yogendra, 1989, Social Stratification and Change in India, New Delhi, Manohar (Reprinted)

Srinivas, M.N., 1952 Religion and Society among the Coorgs of South India, Oxford: Clarendon Press.

Vidyarthi, L.P., 1968, "Cultural Change in the Tribes of Modern India", **Presidential Address** at 55th session of *Indian Science Congress Association*, held in **Varanasi** (Anthropology Section).

Index

Pl. 1 : Mal Paharia House type

Pl. 2 : Mal Paharia mother with her new born

Pl. 3 : Mal Paharia woman involved in household chores

Pl. 4 : Mid day meal of a Mal Paharia family

Pl. 5 : Modern Mal Paharia house under Birsa Abas Yogna

Pl. 6 : Pounding the cereals

Pl. 7 : Preparation of Mahua liquor with indigenous technique

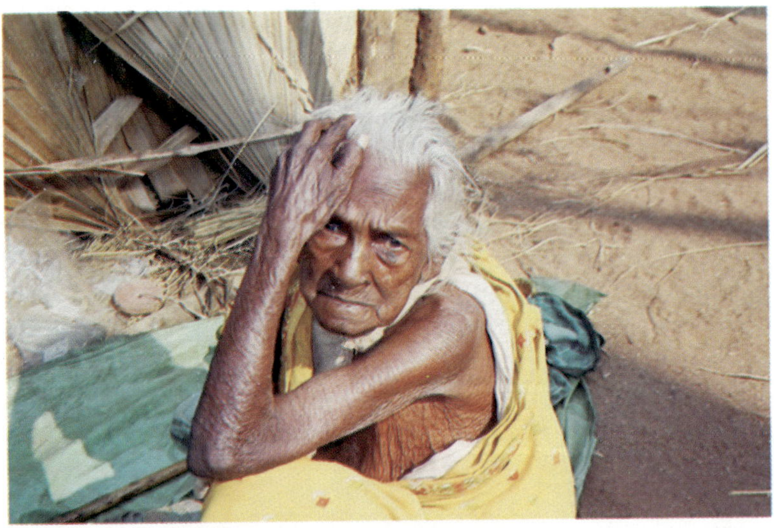

Pl. 8 : Attacked with Baman Jonkh

Pl. 9 : Carrying young log on head - a regular feature for survival

Pl. 10 : Author with villagers at Upar Murgathali village

Pl. 11 : Interviewing group of villagers by one of the author (Samira Dasgupta)

Pl. 12 : Informant Kalicharan Deheri with his wife

Pl. 13 : Ritual Place for Maghi Parab

Pl. 14 : Sacrifice during ritual activities

Pl. 15 : Sal leaves-Collection of Minor forest produce for survival

Pl. 16 : Traditional measuring pot

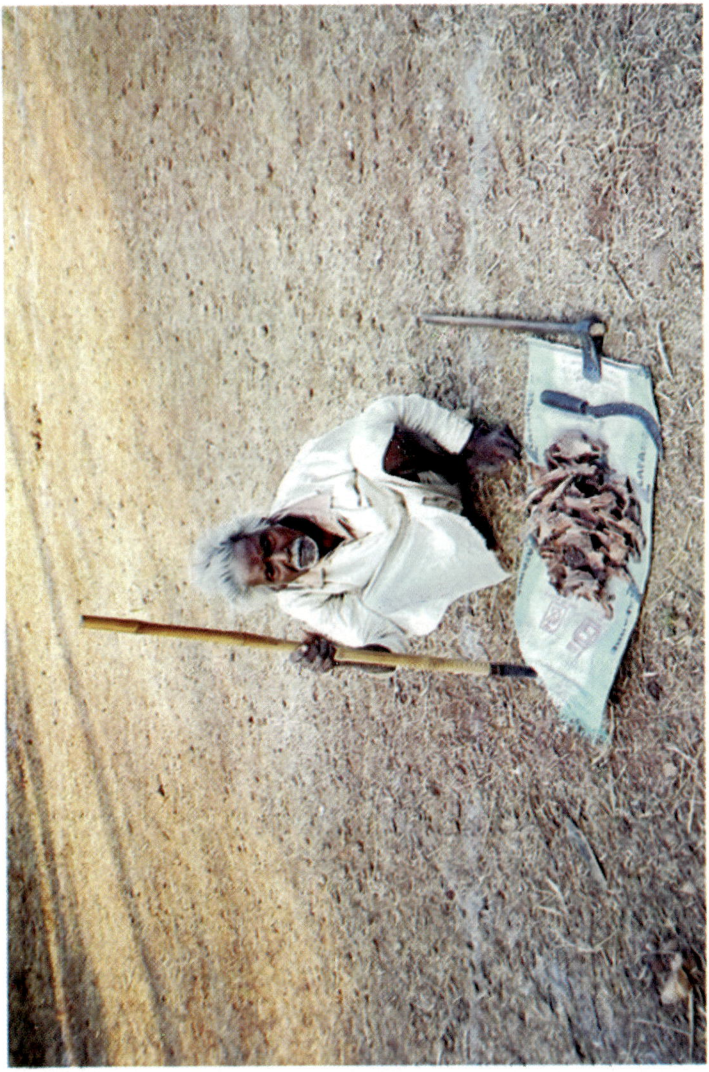

Pl. 17 : Mal Paharia medicineman of Madhuvan village

Pl. 18 : Jonk Cluster in the backyard of Mal Paharia house

Pl. 19 : Community feast after breach of taboo (illicit sex relation between a young widow Mal Paharia)

Pl. 20 : Dilapidated Gando Estate of Mal Paharia

Pl. 21 : Exposed to modernity - an employee of NGO